MAKING [...] N
JIGSAW
PUZZLES

Creating Heirlooms from Photos & Other Favorite Images

by Charles W. Ross

FOX CHAPEL
PUBLISHING

DEDICATION

To my wife, Betty, for her love of puzzles and her
encouragement to buy my first scroll saw and begin making
wooden jigsaw puzzles for our family's enjoyment.

To my father, Charles W. Ross, 3rd, a master puzzle
maker and woodworker who set me on the path
to making wooden jigsaw puzzles.

ISBN 978-1-56523-480-2

Library of Congress Cataloging-in-Publication Data

Ross, Charles W. (Charles Worthington), 1927-
 Making wooden jigsaw puzzles : creating heirlooms from
photos & other favorite images / by Charles W. Ross.
    p. cm.
Includes index.
ISBN 978-1-56523-480-2
1. Woodwork. 2. Jigsaw puzzles. I. Title.
TT180.R67 2010
684'.08--dc22
                        2010031246

To learn more about the other great books from
Fox Chapel Publishing, or to find a retailer near you, call toll-free
800-457-9112 or visit us at *www.FoxChapelPublishing.com*.

Note to Authors: We are always looking for talented authors to write new books in
our area of woodworking, design, and related crafts. Please send a brief letter describing
your idea to Acquisition Editor, 1970 Broad Street, East Petersburg, PA 17520.

Printed in China

First printing: December 2010

CONTENTS

Introduction 8

CHAPTER 1:
Getting Started 10
Equipment 12
Choosing Your Subjects 18
Materials 23
Preparing a Puzzle Blank 26
A Little Philosophy About Making Jigsaw Puzzles . . . 28

CHAPTER 2:
Techniques and Exercises 32
Cutting Jigsaw Puzzle Pieces 34
Problems and Solutions 39
Practice Puzzles 40
Puzzle 1: Strip-Cutting Method 42
Puzzle 2: Sectioning a Puzzle Blank 47
Puzzle 3: Stair-Step Cutting 51
Puzzle 4: Small Freehand Style 55
Puzzle 5: Large Freehand Style 61

CHAPTER 3:
Step-by-Step Projects 68
Jigsaw Puzzle Step-by-Step 70
Boxing Your Puzzle 82

APPENDIX:
A Short History of Jigsaw Puzzles 88
Patterns 93
Index 103

How to Use This Book

This book is chock-full of all the information you'll need
to start creating your very own heirloom wooden jigsaw puzzles.

**Chapter 1: Getting Started
(page 10)** covers the basics of
jigsaw puzzle cutting. You'll learn
what materials and tools you need,
the best sorts of images to choose
as puzzles subjects, how to create
a puzzle blank by joining the image
and the wood, and, finally, some
strategies for planning devious
puzzle pieces.

Chapter 2: Techniques and Exercises (page 32) guides

you through the various cutting methods you'll need to create puzzles. The strip cut, the stair-step cut, sectioning a blank, and other techniques are explained here with detailed step-by-step instructions.

Chapter 3: Step-by-Step Projects (page 68) contains a

fully photographed step-by-step guide to the creation of a full-size heirloom jigsaw puzzle. You'll also find out several options for boxing your puzzle.

Appendix (page 88)

A Short History of Jigsaw Puzzles relates the interesting evolution of jigsaw puzzles. The Patterns section includes 3 practice puzzles for beginners and special templates to add shapes to your puzzles.

Introduction

The first memory I have of seeing a wooden jigsaw puzzle is when I was about six or seven. I wandered into our living room one evening to see my parents and some of their friends huddled around a card table.

As I drew closer, I could see that the table was covered with little odd-shaped colored wood pieces. Everyone was staring at the pieces and picking them up, holding them briefly and putting them down again. Sometimes a person would try to put it down next to another piece.

At first I couldn't figure what they were doing. Also I thought it odd that grownups would all be looking at these strange little pieces with such intense interest. Since this was a grownup evening event, I was hustled off to bed with my mother's quick explanation, "We're just working on a puzzle, dear."

It was only later, when I was older, that my mother allowed me to see a wooden jigsaw puzzle up close. Still, I was mystified that anyone would want to look at all those funny-looking pieces.

As I continued to look at the puzzle, I suddenly got the idea that the goal was to find pieces that fit together. When I was allowed to try, I found it really frustrating. All those irregular shapes made me confused. No piece I could see would fit together with another piece. The irregularly shaped pieces were so small and held such a little bit of color that it was hard to find two to put together.

After some study, though, I managed to put two edge pieces together. I was delighted. Then I found two more pieces that fit into each other.

I was hooked.

As I grew older, I discovered my father was the puzzle maker. Late one warm summer afternoon, I stopped by my father's shop doorway. There was my dad, hunched over a strange piece of machinery. I stopped and watched.

As I approached, I realized my father was using a treadle from an old Singer sewing machine to operate an arm that moved a blade up and down. I watched him move the colored wood against the blade, turning it this way and that. As I came closer, I discovered that the colored wood was actually a picture. He was carefully moving it through the blade. I was amazed. He was actually cutting out a puzzle.

I watched while he carefully cut an intricate shape for a puzzle piece. As he finished each piece, he would pick it up in his fingers, blow the dust off, and place it in a bowl with the other pieces he'd cut. Years later, I learned that during the Depression in the early 1930s, my dad made puzzles to earn extra income.

Putting together a puzzle is a wonderful pastime.

He put his puzzles in bright orange boxes and rented them to friends and acquaintances for $0.25 per week.

When my wife and I lived in Pleasantville, New York, and our four children were young, we rented a Winnebago Brave recreational vehicle and drove it to Disney World. To pass the time while I drove, my wife and our four girls spread out a cardboard 500-piece circular jigsaw puzzle on the dinette table and worked on it during the day. We all have fond memories of that trip and the neat circular puzzle that kept everyone very busy during the long days of driving.

Over the years, I learned that assembling a jigsaw puzzle is a pastime that can be enjoyed with friends and family alike. By reading this book, I hope you will find that making wooden heirloom jigsaw puzzles is an art and a delightful pastime too.

Handmade wooden jigsaw puzzles are sturdy and can be assembled over and over through the years and the pieces feel good in your fingers. The jigsaw puzzles you make will become family heirlooms. Jigsaw puzzles are special unique gifts that the recipient will treasure for a lifetime. An heirloom puzzle will go on giving that same joy of accomplishment year after year.

Making hand-cut wooden jigsaw puzzles is a matter of attention to detail. In this book, I have tried to cover the aspects of basic jigsaw puzzle-making. I will describe the techniques and practice projects necessary to make a beautiful wooden jigsaw puzzle that will give hours of joy to anyone who loves the challenge of solving a puzzle.

Charlie Ross

—Charlie Ross, Belle Haven, Virginia

CHAPTER 1

Getting Started

The old saying goes, "To do anything in woodwork
requires patience and sharp tools." Having the proper
tools and equipment at hand is a necessity in producing
any woodworking project. This is very true of making
heirloom jigsaw puzzles that will be treasured for
generations. In this chapter, we will describe the kinds
of tools, equipment, and materials needed to produce
professional-grade jigsaw puzzles. We'll also discuss
how to choose a jigsaw image, make a puzzle blank, and
everything else you need to know to make your own
jigsaw puzzle.

Learn what wood
and blades to use.

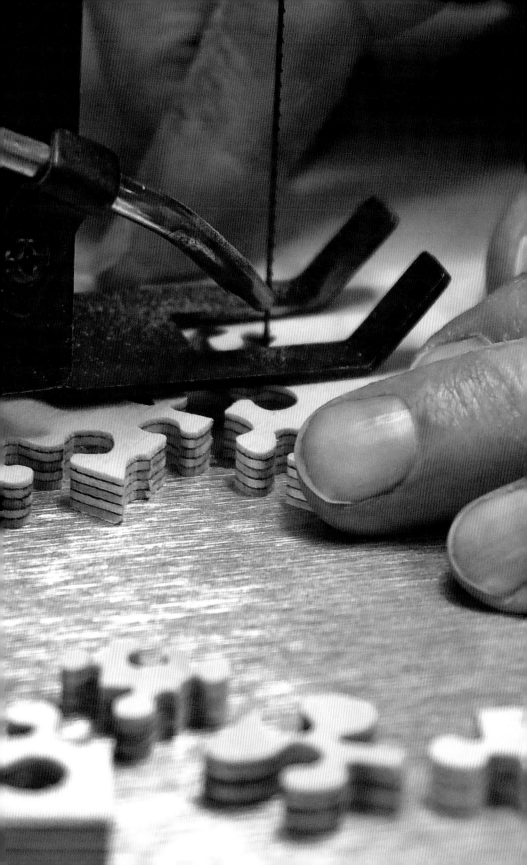

EQUIPMENT

Scroll Saw

Scroll saws come in a variety of sizes and capabilities. One of the most important aspects for puzzle makers is the throat depth. This is the distance from the blade to the front edge of the back frame support. To accommodate puzzles up to about the size of an 8½" x 11" piece of paper, this distance should be at least 16" (406mm).

There are scroll saws with deeper throats and stronger motors, but if cost is a factor in your buying decision, you should consider a variable speed 16" (406mm) machine. With care, you can cut out puzzles up to almost 12" x 16" (305mm x 406mm).

Another feature of scroll saws is single-versus variable-speed motors. For puzzle makers, the variable-speed motor offers the most advantages. The puzzle maker has complete control of the blade speed.

Scroll saw blades.

For example, when you are cutting the last twenty or so pieces from the puzzle blank, the small blank will begin to vibrate. As the last few pieces are cut, the shrinking blank will vibrate up and down with the strokes of the saw and become tough to handle. You can gain control by reducing the rpm of the machine.

Having the ability to gradually reduce the rpm also enables you to carefully cut the last few curves without losing control of the piece. Stroke speeds can be changed to meet the demands of the stock, the thickness of the puzzle blank and the complexity of the piece being cut.

Other important features on a scroll saw include a dust blower and blade tensioner. Be sure the blade meets the table at 90°—vertical cuts make sharp right angle puzzle pieces. Most scroll saws include a foot as standard equipment to hold down the work as the saw cuts.

Even though it's hard to cut the last few puzzle pieces under the foot, I find it to be a useful tool. A pusher stick (as you will see illustrated later on) is a great way to utilize the foot and still have control over those last puzzle pieces.

Blades

After you've purchased a scroll saw, choosing the best blade for the job and your equipment is probably the next

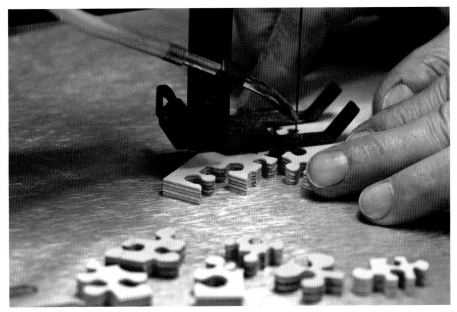

Test scroll saw blades by cutting pieces.

most important decision you'll have to make. It is best to purchase several types of blades from different manufacturers and test them on sample puzzle blanks to determine the blade that works best with the thickness of the stock and the kind of paper being used.

Among the blades you should test are skip tooth and reverse tooth blades. Reverse tooth blades have teeth that are set in two directions to cut smooth edges on the top and bottom of the stock. Skip tooth blades reduce the sawdust buildup and allow smoother cutting at higher rpm. Also keep in mind that the thinnest blade will cut the narrowest space between puzzle pieces, enabling you to

keep most of the puzzle image. Blades that cut cleanly, reduce or eliminate tearout on the bottom of the puzzle piece, and make smooth tight cuts are ideal.

There are many important things to consider when crafting a wooden jigsaw puzzle. None, however, are more critical to the process than a good, sharp, thin saw blade. Smooth graceful cuts are essential to cutting each puzzle piece.

Remember, one of the very tangible things a carefully cut puzzle piece provides is a delightful tactile feel. All sides of the piece must be smooth and carefully shaped. A thin sharp blade running at the right speed accomplishes this goal. Tearout and ragged edges create

A collection of puzzle blanks.

an unsightly appearance before and after the puzzle's assembly. They make the finished puzzle picture hard to see, and require sanding or filing. Needless to say, filing and sanding each individual puzzle piece is a time-consuming and a tiresome process. A good craftsman wants to avoid doing extra work and so will use very sharp scroll saw blades.

For jigsaw puzzles, the blade parameters you need to pay attention to are blade width, blade thickness, and number of teeth per inch (TPI). Thinner blades allow tighter curves. Thus, the tighter the pieces fit, the better the puzzle will look when assembled. The image on the completed puzzle will show nicely without wide gaps between jigsaw puzzle pieces. The greater number of teeth per inch, the smoother the cut.

The trade off in using high TPI blades is a slower feed rate due to sawdust buildup in front of the blade. A higher rpm will clear saw dust faster, but the sacrifice is control of the cut, as the blade will move faster through the stock. A way around this situation is to use a skip tooth blade that has half the number of teeth and can clear the sawdust between teeth easier.

Reverse tooth blades and reverse skip tooth blades cut cleanly on both the up and down stroke. If your stock is too thin, the teeth on the bottom of the blade will cut above the top surface of the stock and produce ragged edges. These blades, however, work fine when the stock is at least ¼" (6mm) thick. Reverse skip tooth blades seem to clear the sawdust faster when cutting at higher strokes per inch (SPI).

What does all this explanation of stock thickness, teeth per inch, and tooth set mean? It means experimentation is very important to determine what type of blade works best on a particular type of scroll saw and stock. The best way to decide is to purchase a pack of blades of each type. Don't buy blades from just one manufacturer either. The better choice is to get different types of blades from at least two or three companies.

Cut five or more practice pieces from your puzzle blank stock with each type of blade you have purchased. Check the smoothness of the cut, examine the amount of tearout, and get the feel of how the stock feeds through the blade. When you're satisfied you have learned all you can about a particular kind of blade from one manufacturer, record your findings. Make notes about the smoothness of the cut, any tearout that appears, the ease of feed, SPI of the machine, and any other remarks. Besides helping you identify the best blades for you, this process will also give you more confidence and understanding of the puzzle making process.

Lighting and Eye Protection

Cutting small jigsaw puzzle pieces requires good clear light on the work. The light should be strong enough to see your work clearly but not so bright as to cause glare and eye strain. A round fluorescent adjustable light works well. A fluorescent bulb costs more than an incandescent bulb but will be more inexpensive to use,

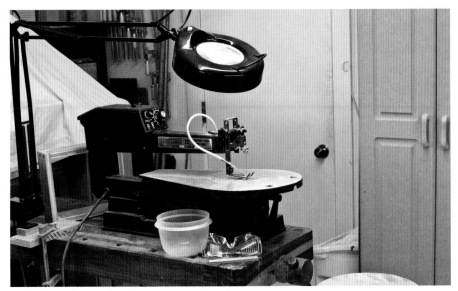

Scroll saw and magnifier light on the workbench.

lasts longer, and is more environmentally friendly. Whatever light is chosen, the light stand must be fully adjustable. The operator must be able to move the light to the best position to reduce glare on the work. Another advantage of a fully adjustable light is it can be moved out of the way for blade changing and vacuuming up sawdust.

The round adjustable fluorescent light usually has a magnifier in the middle. Early in my puzzle making, I decided to use the magnifier in hopes of cutting even smaller puzzle pieces. However, looking through the magnifier at what I was cutting was absolutely disorienting. Also, it turned out that I couldn't cut pieces any smaller, so there was really no payoff for using the magnifier except for making myself uncomfortably dizzy. I do use the magnifier to examine pieces I've cut to see how my blades are wearing as well as for examining new blades.

Wearing eye protection is an important part of operating a scroll saw without injury. Although it is rare, highly tensioned scroll saw blades can fracture. A piece of the blade can break off and fly anywhere. To reduce this risk, as well as increasing the precision of your cutting, change blades often. Dull blades are weak blades.

Seating

Because puzzle makers sit motionless for three quarters of an hour or so at a time, the seat on which one sits becomes a prime consideration. I once sat on a stool with a small wooden seat to cut puzzle pieces. The position and the size of the small oak seat produced exquisite back pain in no time. The puzzle maker needs to be high enough to place their hands comfortably on the scroll saw table and work for a period of time without back strain.

Fatigue is the enemy of the puzzle maker because cutting tiny intricate jigsaw puzzle pieces requires patience

Make sure you have a good stool to use when scrolling.

Make a sieve box to vacuum dust from the puzzle pieces.

and a steady hand to make each piece perfect without an error. Sitting at the correct height on a comfortable seat will delay fatigue and discomfort. Breaks from cutting puzzle pieces must be taken at regular intervals to eliminate errors caused by fatigue.

Other Equipment

There are two other items necessary for making heirloom jigsaw puzzles. One is a bowl to collect the jigsaw puzzle pieces as they are cut from the blank. This bowl or container can be of any material or shape. The other item is a sieve to enable vacuuming of the pieces—sawdust tends to accumulate on the pieces and in the bowl.

Vacuuming would be a great way to clean up the dust, but how do you vacuum off small puzzle pieces without sucking them into the vacuum hose? The solution presented itself when I observed my wife using a sieve to wash vegetables. I combined some plastic screening and a plywood frame to create a sieve to hold puzzle pieces. The frame is made of ¾" (19mm) plywood about 12" (305mm) long per side and 3" (76mm) deep. Fine mesh plastic window screening is stapled to the bottom of this frame. To firmly secure the screen, I screwed ⅜" (10mm)-thick by ¾" (19mm)-wide strips of oak to the bottom of the frame. To use, place the finished puzzle pieces into the sieve box and move the shop vacuum hose over the bottom of the screen. Not all of the sawdust will fall off the puzzle pieces until you've assembled the puzzle at least one time.

CHOOSING YOUR SUBJECTS

Choosing an image is the initial starting point in the design of a challenging and difficult puzzle project. Picking an image for a wooden jigsaw puzzle project requires the balancing of three criteria: intriguing image, appropriate paper weight, and low cost. There are many sources for great puzzle images.

Image

Consider this: jigsaw puzzles should present a high degree of difficulty to the person assembling the puzzle. To create an intriguing jigsaw puzzle, the puzzle maker should select a fascinating image. After all, when selecting a puzzle to put together, don't you look at the image first? What are the criteria for an interesting image that will make a difficult puzzle?

There are two qualities that make an image appropriate to be featured on a jigsaw puzzle: repeating patterns or lots of similar colors. This means that the image can be of anything, but should meet certain standards. The image can be very busy and contain lots of color, activity, and designs, or it can be as simple as a pair of geese on a still pond under a sky filled with fleecy clouds.

If the pieces are cut small enough, both of these images, for different reasons, will present a challenge to the puzzle assembler. In the first case, the

image contains many colors and many subjects, which require the assembler to pay close attention to the image. The second example will have many pieces of the same color, requiring the assembler to examine the shapes of the pieces to put the puzzle together. Thus each jigsaw puzzle, although their images are totally different, will display many confusing similarities.

A picture that contains a variety of patterns, a multitude of subjects, or both, will raise the degree of difficulty for the puzzle assembler and create a beautiful image when assembled. Imagine a field of sunflowers with monarch butterflies flitting among them; a library bookcase loaded with volumes of books; or bicycle racers rounding a bend of a narrow mountain road flanked by cheering fans crowding in along the route. These pictures present complicated scraps of color when cut into small puzzle pieces.

A second option is choosing a close-up image. Imagine a pair of mallard ducks floating on still water; a branch bursting with cherry blossoms floating on the breeze below fleecy clouds; or consider an array of multicolored marbles in a cut-glass water goblet standing on a sunlit mahogany table. These types of images will have many similar colored jigsaw puzzle pieces.

Paper Weight

The other basic criterion for choosing puzzle images is the weight of the paper stock on which the picture is printed. If the paper stock is too heavy, your scroll saw blade will produce ugly, fuzzy edges. Heavy paper also dulls scroll saw blades.

When a blade dulls, it will start producing not only fuzzy edges, but also splinter tearout on the bottom of the puzzle pieces. If this happens, you'll have to use a jeweler's file to smooth out the fuzzy edges, which takes hours. This kind of labor isn't fun. It's not what puzzle making is all about. Thus, it's very important to select a light to medium weight of paper to use for jigsaw puzzles.

Photo paper is measured in millimeters of thickness (abbreviated as mil on the packets). Premium photo paper comes in a thickness of 10 mil or heavier, and produces disastrous results when making puzzle pieces. An everyday, less-expensive photo paper is thinner and very suitable for cutting small jigsaw puzzle pieces. Choose digital photo paper no thicker than 8.0 to 8.5 mil. My choice of photo paper is 6.5 mil thick. The thinner the paper, the cleaner it will cut.

Sources

There are plenty of good sources of cheap images for puzzles if you know where to look. Bookstores have sales on old books and calendars, and books they wish to clear out for whatever reason. Both used and discount bookstores are wonderful resources for coffee table books, road atlases, and last year's calendars. Your friends and neighbors are a great source of free images. Let them know you are looking for old calendars, magazine and catalog covers, and posters. You'll be amazed what will be offered to you.

Note: If you are intending to create wooden jigsaw puzzles for sale and

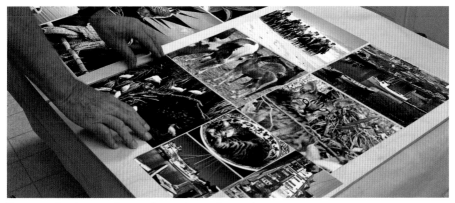

Here are a few images that can be used to make puzzles.

Heirloom Puzzle Image Ideas

Birds	Landscapes
Cats	Children
Dogs	Fantasy
Owls	
Wolves	Maps
Horses	Nature
Religious scenes	Wildlife
Christmas scenes	People
Flowers	Insects
Botanical scenes	Manufacturing
Cityscapes	Trains
American life	Planes
European life	Sailboats
Oriental life	Powerboats
Sea life	Automobiles
Primitive art	Holidays
Folk art	Gardens
Sports	Food
Military	Wine
Abstracts	Cartoons
Still life	

you decide to use images from books, calendars, or any copyrighted source, it is best to obtain the copyright holder's authorization to use the copyrighted image in commerce.

Calendars are an excellent source for puzzle pictures. The trick is to buy the calendar you want at the end of the year; the price will be discounted to half or less of the original price. Better yet, go to a used or discount bookstore and find outdated calendars. Don't forget to ask your friends and neighbors for their old calendars.

Photographs are a great source of images for puzzles, especially with the advent of digital photos. Any family photo, either color or black and white, is an excellent subject source. A jigsaw puzzle of the family pet will provide delight to younger family members. With today's excellent photo printers and computer software, you can make digital photos of any size you wish.

Doing the prints yourself gives you more control over the subject matter and the weight of the photo paper you use (remember, thinner not heavier). There are inexpensive photo printers that make excellent photos up to 8.5 x 11" (216mm x 279mm). To make larger prints than letter size, a more expensive large-bed photo printer is needed.

If you own a computer and a flat bed image scanner, you can scan any image—something you don't want to cut out of a book, an image on thick paper, a small image you want to resize—into a file. From that, you can print any size print you desire, and on the appropriate paper thickness.

Use acid-free photo paper and pigmented ink, if possible, to lengthen the life of your puzzles. The wrinkle here is that pigmented ink is used almost exclusively in high-end professional printers. Liquid non-pigmented inks can fade over time when exposed to light for extended periods.

Usually, puzzles are only exposed for several days or a week while being assembled, so this isn't a real issue, but it is something to be aware of. If the photo jigsaw puzzle is placed in a good wooden or pasteboard box and assembled once or twice a year, it should last quite a long time without fading. Using pigmented inks on acid-free photo paper will just make the image last a lifetime.

Posters are usually made on heavier paper stock and may not be suitable for jigsaw puzzle use, but posters on lighter paper stock make excellent puzzle blanks. It takes time to find a good inexpensive source of posters. If you wish to make 11" x 14" (279mm x 356mm) or larger puzzles and have the equipment to handle such a large puzzle, then posters are the way to go. It's fun to make a big puzzle.

Magazine and catalog covers without too much printing are great for puzzles. Covers usually have interesting photographs or drawings. Catalog covers also have appeal, providing the subject depicted on the cover is exciting or intricate. Always check the creativity in the cover design and the weight of the paper stock. Use the cover of a college alumni magazine as a gift for a present, past, or future student of that school. Choose a woodworking tool catalog for a puzzle destined for a woodworker—the possibilities are endless.

Lithographs are high-quality prints made on medium- to heavy-weight paper. They can be excellent sources for puzzles. The cost is usually the sticking point with using these wonderful prints. Bargains can be discovered in yard sales and on the Internet. As usual, check the weight of the paper to assure that it is light enough to make a jigsaw puzzle blank.

Maps were the first puzzle subjects, and continue to make a wonderful jigsaw puzzle subject. A good map to use is one that is flat, without creases. An excellent source for interesting maps is a standard road atlas. An atlas from previous years can probably be found at a bargain price at discount stores. Friends may have an old road atlas that you could have, so ask around. A road atlas is usually at least 12" x 16" (305mm x 406mm) in size, so it can be cut to any size you wish. Instead of making a puzzle blank that is rectangular, make the edge conform to the boundary of the particular state, island, or landmass you are using for your subject. By cutting around the boundary, there will be no straight edges to this puzzle. It's well worth the effort to search out an old map reproduction. Remember, if the paper is too heavy, scan it and reprint.

Coffee table books are an interesting source of pictures for puzzles. You can buy out-of-date books at used or discount bookstores for a fraction of the cost of the item when it was new. Many are 11" x 14" (279mm x 356mm) or larger. The choices of subject matter are endless, and the cost per picture is probably the lowest of any source. You can find books of paintings by contemporary or old masters, sports photographs, landscapes, and photographs of people. Keep in mind the heavier the paper the more chance it will leave ragged edges when cut.

Puzzle blanks can be made from digital photos you have taken.

MATERIALS

We've already given a lot of thought to the most visual aspect of a jigsaw puzzle: the image. Now I'll discuss what materials you need for the rest of the puzzle, including glue and backing materials.

Backing Materials

About 100 years ago, puzzle makers had well-dried, wide planks of hardwoods available to them. Nowadays, purchased boards need to sit for a few years to ensure their dryness. If not, you risk having the wood warp—which would ruin your puzzle. Today, the backing material of choice for making wooden heirloom jigsaw puzzle blanks is dimensionally stable plywood. Even in thin sheets, plywood remains flat and will not twist when run through a table saw. To make plywood, thin sheets of wood are glued together, alternating grain direction by 90°, with moisture resistant or waterproof adhesives.

Plywood comes in many sizes, numbers of plys, and grades. Plywood can be purchased in sheets from 6" x 12" (152mm x 305mm) up to 48" x 96" (1219mm x 2438mm) and beyond. Most of the large 4' x 8' (1.2m x 2.4m) three-, four-, or five-ply sheets are AD grade. This means that there is a perfect (A) side, and an imperfect (D) side. On the D side, there may be knots

Plywood works very well for puzzle making.

and imperfections in the surface. To use this material for puzzle blanks, the woodworker must correct the imperfections with wood putty or plastic wood to make the surface smooth and acceptable. A more efficient approach is to select smaller sheets of plywood with AA surfaces. This means the surfaces of both sides are perfect, with no knots or imperfections.

A good choice for a backing material for the puzzle blanks is five-ply, ¼" (6mm)-thick marine plywood in a 24" x 30" (610mm x 762mm) sheet. This material uses waterproof glue and has good stability, and puzzle pieces cut from it feel good in your fingers when you pick them up. A ⁵⁄₃₂" (4mm)-thick sheet is another good choice for puzzle making; however, it only has three plies.

Glues

There are several types of glues used for attaching the puzzle image to the puzzle backing material. For making multiple blanks at one time, there are two kinds of adhesive that work well in joining puzzle images to the plywood blank. One is contact cement and the other is wood glue. For making a single puzzle blank, I recommend a spray adhesive. Do not use rubber cement.

Yellow or white wood glue can be used to cement the picture to the plywood blank. Use a disposable brush to spread the glue evenly over the wood blank. Carefully place the puzzle image on the wood surface. Use a good clean roller to squeeze out the bubbles from the surface.

Next, clamp the puzzle blank flat until the glue dries. A large clamping press is used to maintain the flatness of the surface. A good press will have clamps on each side and a series of thick boards running across from one side to the other side. Also, the clamping press must be larger than the biggest puzzle you plan to make.

Place a sheet of waxed paper over the picture so that any squeeze-out will not adhere the paper to the pressboard. You can press several blanks at once—just be sure to put waxed paper between them. Leave the puzzle blank in the press for about 24 hours to assure that the glue dries completely.

Contact cement is a strong adhesive that is used to fasten down laminate

Here, I'm preparing to make puzzle blanks by laying out pictures on plywood sheets.

onto countertops. When using this adhesive for puzzles, no clamping press is required. Brush both the wood surface and the paper image with a light coat of contact cement.

When the adhesive-covered surfaces are dry to the touch (10–15 minutes), carefully join the two surfaces: place an edge of the picture against the edge of the blank. With these edges straight, smooth the picture slowly to the opposite side of the blank using a roller. Make sure there are no bubbles. Beware of using old contact cement—if too much solvent has evaporated, the adhesive will cause problems with cutting the puzzle. Buy new contact cement if in doubt.

Spray adhesive is a good choice for making one or two puzzle blanks at a time. Look for a spray adhesive that states on the label that it's OK for photo papers. Use a vacuum and a tack rag to remove all the sawdust from the face of the plywood board.

To prevent the image from flying away and landing on a glue surface, wrap a small piece of painter's tape in a ring so the sticky side is out. Put one side against the image and the other against a piece of newspaper or brown paper. This way the image will stay put while you spray. Also place the plywood on a clean sheet of paper. At the distance indicated on the

adhesive label, spray a light coat of adhesive on both surfaces.

After the spraying is completed, wait the prescribed time for a double bond and carefully place the photo on the plywood board. Begin at one corner and slowly lay the photo down onto the plywood, working from one side to the other. After the photo is down on the plywood, use a clean roller to assure there are no bubbles remaining between the surfaces.

Rubber cement should not be considered for making puzzle blanks. Rubber cement contains a solvent that has high penetrating qualities. The solvent dries quite rapidly and can produce gummy globs on the surface. Because of the solvent, the cement may penetrate the paper and mar the image.

Paper/glue compatability is an important consideration. The paper that usually gives the best results is coated paper. Upscale magazines, coffee table books, photo paper, and good-quality calendars use coated papers. Coated paper has a slick glossy or semi-glossy surface and is quite smooth to the touch. By selecting coated paper, you can be reasonably certain that contact cement, wood glue, or spray adhesive will not penetrate the paper and mar the image. To be sure, make a test piece with the same materials to be used to make the puzzle blank.

PREPARING A PUZZLE BLANK

Here, I'll explain step-by-step how to
create many puzzle blanks at one time.
By assembling puzzle blanks in a batch
process, you can make 15 to 18 blanks
at once. This gives you a good supply of
puzzle blanks and a selection of images
from which to choose for your next
heirloom jigsaw puzzle project.

There's a sense of satisfaction that
follows the completion of a group of
puzzle blanks. It is only a part of the
process, but still it's satisfying to know
there is a supply of finished puzzle
blanks all ready to go. The puzzle blanks
can be stored in a drawer or a cabinet in
a very dry area. The making of puzzle
blanks is not an end in itself, but still
there's a feeling of accomplishment in
their completion.

Sizing a puzzle blank

When you begin to make a jigsaw
puzzle, the first step is to cut the puzzle
in half. Thus, it's vital to know how large
a jigsaw puzzle the throat of your scroll
saw will accept. The puzzle blank is the
correct size for your scroll saw when the
distance from the center of the longest
side to the opposite corner will clear the
back of the throat.

For example, say you are making a 12"
x 16" (305mm x 406mm) puzzle. The
long side is 16" (406mm). The center of
that side is at the 8" (203mm) mark. A
measurement line from that point to the
opposite corner of the 12" (305mm) side
is a diagonal of some 14.25" (362mm).
If you are using a scroll saw with a 16"
(406mm) throat, you will clear that
corner as you make your first cut and be
able to cut the puzzle blank in half.

PREPARING A PUZZLE BLANK

MATERIALS

- [ ] A clamping press larger than the largest puzzle blank (for wood glue)
- [ ] One or more sheets of ¼" (6mm) five-ply or thinner plywood
- [ ] Selected puzzle pictures trimmed to size
- [ ] A new container of contact cement or a bottle of white/yellow wood glue
- [ ] Waxed paper (for wood glue)
- [ ] 2" (51mm) disposable bristle brush
- [ ] Roller
- [ ] Pencil
- [ ] Straight edge
- [ ] Paper towels for cleanup
- [ ] Table saw, jigsaw, or portable circular saw (or have the lumberyard cut blanks)

1 **Select images that fit on the plywood.** You can save money and time by purchasing large sheets of plywood, attaching multiple images, and then cutting the puzzle blanks apart with a saw. Start with at least one 24" x 36" (610mm x 914mm) piece of ¼" (6mm)-thick five-ply plywood. Lay out several puzzle pictures to fit over the entire surface.

2 **Mark the spot where each puzzle picture rests.** Number the blank and the back of the corresponding picture. With your straight edge, draw the outlines of the pictures on the plywood.

3 **Using your saw of choice, cut out the blanks.**

4 **Sand off the saw marks and rough edges at the corners.**

5 **Attach the images to the plywood.** Follow the directions for gluing on pages 24–25. Be sure to use a clamping press for wood glue. After the blank and the image are fastened together, wait at least 24 hours for the glue to dry thoroughly.

6 **Sand the edges.** Use a sanding block or a disc sander to smooth the edges of the puzzle to assure that they are clear of glue and the image is not hanging over the edge.

7 **Name the puzzle.** On the back of each puzzle blank, write the name of the puzzle. The name can be the painting's name and artist, the title from the calendar, or one you have made up yourself.

A LITTLE PHILOSOPHY ABOUT MAKING JIGSAW PUZZLES

My personal philosophy on puzzles is to make them so they present a very high degree of difficulty and interest. I use as many tricks as I can to confound the person who tries to assemble a puzzle I have made. My goal is to make the puzzle assembler work hard to connect each piece.

When a puzzle is tough to assemble, it is more satisfying and fun. People will remember and talk about a difficult puzzle. They will fondly discuss the tricks a tough jigsaw puzzle presented. They will go back time and time again to assemble it with their friends. Over the years, this difficult, interesting jigsaw puzzle eventually becomes a favorite family heirloom.

There are many techniques one can use to confound a puzzle assembler. The following methods are ones that, taken together in a single jigsaw puzzle, will make the assembly quite tough. These techniques make a memorable jigsaw puzzle.

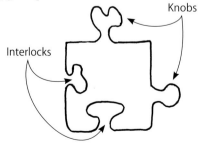

Diagram of a jigsaw puzzle piece.

Add Interlocking Tabs

The first wooden jigsaw puzzles didn't employ pieces that were cut to interlock together—they were just shapes that fit against each other. However, interlocking each puzzle piece with another brings a new and more intriguing aspect to assembling jigsaw puzzles. These knobs and interlocks add more complexity to the shape of each puzzle piece. Each knob is cut to fit only into its mating interlock. When many puzzle pieces look exactly the same, finding that unique mate is more difficult than just trying to slide a flat side against another flat side.

Obscure or Hide the Edge Pieces

Disguising the edge of a puzzle will confuse those who start a puzzle by trying to fit the edge pieces together first. This can be done in several ways. One way is to cut the edge into an irregular shape (see the photograph at right top, piece #1). Another way is to cut the edge with interlocking shapes so as to resemble an interior puzzle piece, as in piece fourteen.

Hide the Corners

There are several ways to hide a corner. One method is to cut a 45° angle at the corner (see pieces #10 and 11 in the photograph at right). Note the interlock between these two parts is on the diagonal. Another way to disguise a corner is to round the puzzle corner (#1). The corner rounding is done when the puzzle blank is made. To complete the illusion cut one or two false interlocks in the rounded corner to make this piece look like an interior puzzle piece. Another way is to take a perfectly good right-angled corner and cut one interlock into one straight side. Now you have made the corner piece take on the aspect of an edge piece (#4).

Embed Fancy Figures in the Puzzle Design

Cutting fancy figures in a jigsaw puzzle first started in the early 1900s, when puzzle makers would cut birds, butterflies, fish, initials, animals, or other figures into their jigsaw puzzles. This technique creates interest and fun for the puzzle assembler. These pieces don't necessarily make the puzzle more difficult, because each of these figures has an edge that the puzzle assembler can use to fit pieces together. If the fancy figure is large enough, however, it can be cut into several smaller puzzle pieces to add difficulty. The photograph at right has examples of several fancy shape templates that are used to embed figures into the interior of a jigsaw puzzle.

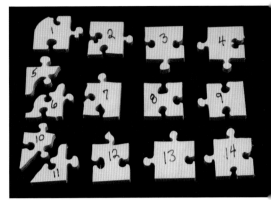
Examples of interlocking pieces unassembled.

Drawing figure designs can be a problem if you're not good at drawing free hand. There is a way around this dilemma—use stencils. The Internet is a good place to look for free stencils. Print these figures and reduce them on a copy machine as necessary to fit the size puzzle blank you are using. Glue the paper outlines on plywood and cut them out for use as templates. This way the figure can be used for other puzzles.

Examples of fancy embedded figure templates.

Make an Irregular Puzzle Shape

Many jigsaw puzzles are made either in a square or a rectangular shape. Unless the edge pieces are disguised, finding edge pieces is somewhat straightforward. If a puzzle is made with an irregular shape, finding the edge pieces is a little more difficult. Imagine a large puzzle made from a photo of an eagle, without a background, where the border of the puzzle is the outline of the eagle. This irregular shape makes finding the edges of such a puzzle much more difficult.

Cut Unique Interlocks

The photo on page 31 shows examples of various shapes of interlocks. This figure demonstrates some of the various types of puzzle pieces that can be cut from a square shape. It isn't necessary to follow a square shape when cutting free hand— any shape will be just fine. Keep in mind the more shapes that look the same, the more confusing the jigsaw puzzle will become. Making unique interlocks is fun and adds interest. This technique can also give the puzzle assembler some pieces that are easy to find and connect. It is fun, however, to select one special interlock shape as a kind of signature and use it several times.

Cut Out Shapes from Inside the Puzzle and Leave Them Out

The term for this technique is drop outs. Cutting drop outs requires careful planning—you must select a picture that lends itself to this technique. For example, consider a picture of a house on a hill with a barn and several trees under a blue sky. After the blank is made, cut out and remove some clouds from the sky. Suppose there are tiny parts of the interior of the picture that can be removed. These can be doors or windows or other items that have unique shapes. The drop outs create extra edge pieces and an unusually shaped puzzle.

Cut Along the Color Lines

This is an easy technique. As you cut out puzzle pieces, find spots in the puzzle that separate one color from another. These can be edges of color, such as the petals of a flower or the edge of a hand. When the two color edges are separated, the connection is divorced and makes it difficult to find pieces that match up. When adjoining pieces don't have scraps of color to give away their locations, they are overlooked as candidates for the connecting puzzle pieces. Any object in the puzzle with an edge of a different color is a candidate for this technique.

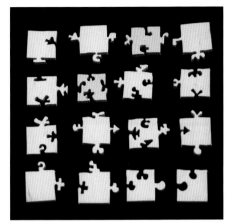

Interlocking edge puzzle shapes.

Cut Pieces that Resemble Each Other

Cut pieces so they have the same shape. For example, cut puzzle pieces with two knobs and two interlocks that look exactly alike. Doing this makes the shape and look of each puzzle piece similar. If they are also the same color, so much the better!

Cut Smaller Pieces

The smaller a puzzle piece is cut, the harder it is to find where it goes. Remember, smaller pieces have fewer details and colors to indicate how they connect with other pieces. The downside to this is there is a limit to how small a piece you can cut without error.

Make Faux Edge Pieces Out of Interior Pieces

To confuse those who start to assemble a jigsaw puzzle by connecting all the edge pieces first, make extra, or false, edge pieces. When cutting the interior puzzle pieces of the jigsaw puzzle blank, cut a very straight side without interlocks. If the colors are close to those of the real edge pieces, the result will be interior pieces that resemble edge pieces. This will create some confusion for the puzzle assembler.

There are always ways to improve on these techniques. As you cut jigsaw puzzles, you'll discover clever variations to these methods and soon your puzzles will take on a unique quality. These unique and difficult jigsaw puzzles will become treasured heirlooms by all who are lucky enough to have the pleasure to assemble them.

CHAPTER 2
Techniques and Exercises

Cutting jigsaw puzzle pieces is a very precise process where there can be no mistakes. Each puzzle piece must be cut carefully without errors. Cutting practice puzzle pieces from a practice blank is a good way to get started making error-free jigsaw puzzle pieces. Think of it this way: before playing a round, a golfer goes to the practice range to limber up and hit a few balls. A baseball pitcher warms up in the bullpen before pitching in a game. The same is true with a puzzle maker. Cutting pieces from a practice blank builds confidence and dexterity.

Cutting puzzle pieces from a practice blank.

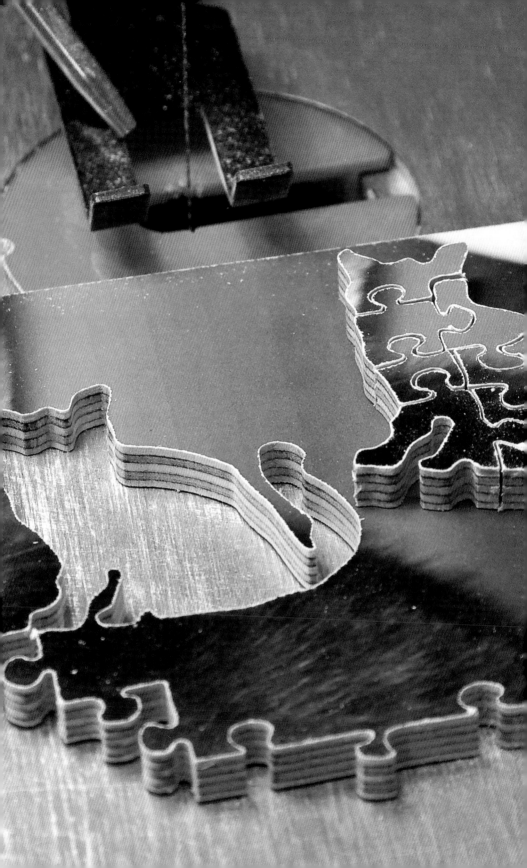

CUTTING JIGSAW PUZZLE PIECES

Cutting jigsaw puzzle pieces is the exciting part of the process. Cutting a piece requires intense concentration and care by the puzzle maker. There can be no mistakes. Each puzzle piece must be cut perfectly. This simple requirement puts a little stress on the puzzle maker.

The rule, as in most woodworking projects, is to use a slow smooth motion to fashion graceful curves. A smooth, gentle pressure on the puzzle blank as the blade cuts delivers a glossy surface to the piece. This is what makes a wooden jigsaw puzzle piece feel so delightful in your fingers.

to 45 minutes or so, take a break. Resist making those one or two extra jigsaw puzzle pieces. Instead, go work on the puzzle box for the jigsaw puzzle you are making. This is always a satisfying task, especially if the jigsaw puzzle is a gift.

The time away from the scroll saw will drain away the tension and give your muscles a relaxing change. After twenty minutes to a half hour of doing something else, go back and spend another 30 to 45 minutes constructing beautiful jigsaw puzzle pieces. You'll be refreshed and ready to cut some exciting shapes.

Fatigue

Because making jigsaw puzzle pieces requires a high degree of concentration, you need to set a pace that is comfortable and take frequent rest breaks. This is where patience plays a big part. There is always a tendency to forge ahead and make just a few more jigsaw puzzle pieces rather than take a rest. Fatigue is a very gradual condition. Most of us cannot tell when we are more tired than we were twenty minutes ago. This is where the possibility of an error in cutting is the greatest.

In jigsaw puzzle making, each puzzle piece must be crafted perfectly. After cutting jigsaw puzzle pieces for about 30

Blades

As you begin to cut practice pieces, closely examine a few to determine if the blade is becoming dull and needs replacing. Look for clean cuts and no rough or torn paper edges. It's a good idea to begin each puzzle-making session with a new scroll saw blade.

When you replace a dull scroll saw blade with a new sharp blade, the work will feed easier and cut faster. The new scroll saw blade will cut with the slightest pressure. Extra care needs to be taken when cutting the first several puzzle pieces with a new scroll saw blade.

Reduce the speed when using a fresh blade to make it cut slower and minimize over cutting. Cutting practice puzzle pieces with a fresh blade will provide experience with how fast the blade will cut at various speeds.

Choosing a blank

To choose a jigsaw puzzle blank, you should ask several questions. Where is this puzzle going? Is it a gift? If so who is the recipient? Will they like the chosen subject, or would another subject be a better choice? When it's finished, will this jigsaw puzzle be offered for sale? Is it for your personal enjoyment as part of your collection of jigsaw puzzles? The answers to these questions determine the subject to choose.

Look at the title written on the puzzle's back. Make a note of the jigsaw puzzle title on your clipboard, project notebook, or on a sheet of paper. The title and the number of puzzle pieces, along with the creation date and your name, will be written on the puzzle box. Doing it this way is orderly and helps the project go smoothly.

After the jigsaw puzzle blank is selected, the next step is getting the workshop ready. Set up your scroll saw. Attach the adjustable light to the bench and assemble the rest of the puzzle-making equipment and supplies. When all is ready, it is time to begin the project.

Examples of the shapes of various puzzle pieces.

Visualizing a Space

When preparing to cut a jigsaw puzzle piece, you must look at the area of the puzzle blank from which the piece is to be cut. There is a decision to be made at this point. Visualizing how a piece will look is an important aspect of cutting puzzle pieces freehand. Though each piece can be unique, the more pieces look the same, the more the entire puzzle will confuse the assembler.

In what direction will the interlocks go? A jigsaw puzzle piece is usually square or oblong, with interlocks on all four sides. To make an interlock into a puzzle piece, there must be space to accommodate it; otherwise, the interlock should be cut into the

Locating a fancy figure on the puzzle blank.

Interlocks

Each piece is cut so it will fit, or interlock, into the other pieces. This means that if the piece is somewhat square, there will be an interlock on each side. Cutting puzzle pieces freehand will seldom produce exactly square puzzle pieces, but the idea is to have each piece interlock with its neighbor.

Experiment with different styles of interlocks—you'll have many to cut on a puzzle, so you'd better start building up your repertoire now! The important thing is to make sure the head of the key is larger than the neck. The pieces fit together better that way. Beyond that, the shape of the pieces is up to you.

You will cut at least four knobs and/or interlocks out of each jigsaw puzzle adjoining puzzle piece. There are various ways to combine knobs and interlocks. Some pieces have four internal interlocks while others have two knobs and two interlocks. There's no hard and fast rule—knobs and interlocks can be made anywhere.

Fancy figure drawn on the puzzle blank.

The shape of the cat has been cut out.

piece. This is a process that will be repeated over and over again. Cutting knobs is the time where the risk of an error is the highest. The knob or interlock is wider at the head of the knob than it is nearer the body of the puzzle piece. This makes the pieces interlock with one another.

The neck of the knob can cut too narrow, making it prone to breakage. There needs to be sufficient wood in the neck of the knob to support the knob for reassembly. Practice puzzles come into good use for testing how narrow a neck can be and still be substantial enough to get assembled over and over.

Though you can cut simple knobs and interlocks, creative interlocking knobs can be fun to make. The pieces shown in the photo on page 31 demonstrate various shapes of creative interlocks. Distinctive shapes add excitement for the assembler.

Remember, however, there is a trade-off when constructing decorative or distinctive knobs. When knobs are unique, their fancy shapes are a giveaway. The assembler can easily find the matching piece. Making two or more of the same distinctive knob shape can diminish this effect.

Another use for the distinctive decorative knob can be as the maker's personal signature. A creatively cut, distinctive knob will stand out from other knobs on other pieces. Some makers cut their initials into the puzzle, while others create a fancy figure to identify themselves.

The more smooth, rounded knobs that are cut with the same shape, the harder the jigsaw puzzle will be. For example, cutting two smooth, rounded knobs and two carefully cut interlocks exactly in the same position on a hundred small jigsaw puzzle pieces presents the assembler with many puzzle pieces that look identically like each other. This can make assembly quite demanding.

Fancy Figures

In Chapter 1, we discussed methods and techniques of adding difficulty to jigsaw puzzles. Among the techniques discussed was embedding fancy shapes into a puzzle.

There are at least two techniques for cutting out these figures. One method is to make a design on tracing paper and, using painter's tape, adhere the figure to the puzzle board in the desired location. There is a risk involved in this technique in that the tape may adhere too securely to the puzzle picture and mar the picture when removed.

You can also make templates and trace the design on the back of the puzzle. Just be careful when cutting that you don't rip the image on the front. You can either attach your figure patterns to the blank first and cut to them, or just start cutting and add one when it feels right. You can cut the fancy shape into multiple puzzle pieces to disguise it, or leave it intact if you want to give the assembler a leg up.

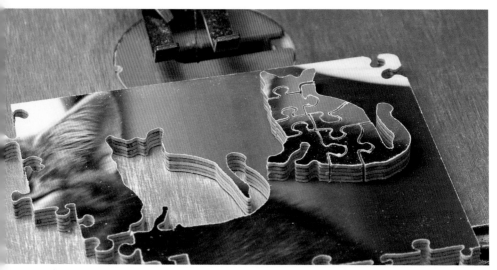

The cat shape has been cut into eight smaller pieces to hide the fancy shape.

PROBLEMS AND SOLUTIONS

Woodworking is all about solving problems and overcoming small mistakes. Even for the most careful and dedicated puzzle maker, there will always be a problem, or a challenge, that will present itself. There are some materials and tools that the puzzle maker should have close at hand for when these little situations present themselves.

Glue and a Toothpick

Sometimes when the scroll saw blade exits a cut at the edge of the puzzle blank, a tiny sliver of wood will separate from the rest of the edge and be held in place only by the image paper. When this happens, carefully lift the broken sliver and use a toothpick and a tiny drop of wood glue to affix the sliver back in place. Have a heavy piece of wood handy to place on top of the jigsaw puzzle piece to hold the sliver in place until the glue dries. Always take care that the weight and the top of the piece have no glue on them.

Large Nail Clippers

This is an odd, but very handy, tool for puzzle makers. On many occasions, the saw will leave little splinters of wood when exiting a cut. To square off these unsightly splinters, use the nail clippers to snip off the edge smoothly and neatly. Don't be tempted to use small nail clippers. Large nail clippers have a wider cutting surface and are bigger and easier to handle than smaller nail clippers.

¼" (6mm) Bristle Brush

This is another very handy little tool. To determine if your blade is getting dull, brush away the fine sawdust from the cut edge of a jigsaw puzzle piece and, under a magnifying glass, inspect the edge. If the paper edge is beginning to look frayed or ragged it is time to replace the scroll saw blade.

Magnifier

The best hands-free way to inspect freshly cut pieces is under a circular fluorescent work light with a magnifier in the center. The lighted magnifier will allow the careful inspection of scroll saw blades and any other need for a magnified image.

PRACTICE PUZZLES

Now we are going to get into the real craft of making wooden jigsaw puzzles. There are five jigsaw puzzle projects in the following pages. They increase in difficulty in order to put into practice the information that has been covered in the previous sections. The first three projects are devoted to learning how to cut smaller and smaller puzzle pieces. The last two projects put all the information in the previous sections to use in making two jigsaw puzzle projects. Each of these project exercises result in a usable jigsaw puzzle. When you complete these five projects, you'll have a better understanding of how to go about making small precise jigsaw puzzle pieces that will feel delightful in the fingers but supply only a scrap of information to the puzzle assembler.

¼" (6mm) plywood puzzle blanks.

Materials & Preparation

For the practice puzzle projects, assemble the following materials:

For stock, we will use ¼" (6mm)-thick 5-ply basswood marine-grade plywood. Marine-grade plywood is a very stable material, cuts easily, and produces smooth-edged puzzle pieces.

- (3) ¼" (6mm)-thick 5" x 7" (127mm x 178mm) 5-ply exterior-grade plywood board
- (1) ¼" (6mm)-thick 5" x 7½" (127mm x 191mm) 5-ply exterior-grade plywood board
- (1) ¼" (6mm)-thick 8" x 10" (203mm x 254mm) 5-ply exterior-grade plywood board
- (5) Small containers for the finished practice puzzle projects. These can be plastic food containers purchased at the grocery store or small boxes.
- Fine sandpaper
- Tack rag
- Spray can of adhesive suitable to adhere a digital photograph to the plywood puzzle blank
- Light shade of oil- or water-based stain
- Spray, brush, or wipe-on finish
- (1) borderless digital photograph, 5" x 7" (127mm x 178mm)
- (1) borderless digital photograph, 8" x 10" (203mm x 254mm)

Two-plywood puzzle boards and two digital images.

The puzzle project containers.

PUZZLE 1: STRIP-CUTTING METHOD

Cutting pieces row by row is a technique called strip cutting. You've seen commercial puzzles made from thick cardboard—these are strip-cut puzzles. For this project, we will strip-cut 1" (25mm) pieces using guidelines. There are two basic steps to strip cutting.

1. Draw guidelines. Draw parallel pencil lines about 1" (25mm) apart in one direction. Draw another set of lines at 90° to the first set. This creates small squares about 1" (25mm) wide.

2. Cut pieces. Cut interlocking puzzle pieces using these precise lines as guides.

Strip-cutting method.

PUZZLE ONE: Strip Cutting

1 Set up. Set up your scroll saw with a new saw-blade, adjustable fluorescent light, a stool of proper height, a bowl to receive the cut puzzle pieces, a small ½" (13mm) brush, a guide stick for cutting the last few pieces, safety glasses, and the sieve to vacuum off the sawdust.

2 Prepare the blank. Select one 5" x 7" (127mm x 178mm) puzzle blank and draw pencil lines 1" (25mm) apart across the 7" (178mm) side of the blank. Repeat along the 5" (127mm) side. This divides the blank into a grid with 1" (25mm) squares.

3 Finish the face of the blank. Vacuum the surface of the blank to clean off any loose sawdust. Use a tack-rag to wipe the surface to remove all remaining sawdust. If you wish, tint the surface with diluted oil or water-based stain of a light color. After the stain has dried overnight, use a tack-rag on the surface again. Apply spray lacquer, acrylic, or any finish you would like to use. Once the finish is dry you are ready to begin.

4 Cut the first piece. Make the first piece at a corner. It is my habit to start on the right corner of a puzzle and strip cut pieces from right to left. If you want to start differently, that's OK.

PUZZLE ONE: Strip Cutting *(continued)*

5 Cut the second piece. Cut piece number two, making knobs and interlocks on all three sides. Remember to cut slowly and carefully with a light touch on the work.

6 Complete the first strip. Continue to cut along the strip, cutting pieces three, four, and five. Along the way you should make a fancy knob or two. As you cut the next puzzle pieces, visualize what each piece will look like before you actually cut. Plan where the knobs and interlocks will face and decide how much room you need for each knob and interlock.

7 Cut the second row. You do not have to follow the lines exactly. By this time, you have discovered that cutting 1" (25mm)-sized pieces is not really difficult. That's true. What you need to learn here is that pre-planning is necessary before cutting each piece. This knowledge will be invaluable when you start cutting very small puzzle pieces.

Tip: Take a Break

Remember, every 30 to 45 minutes or so take a break from cutting pieces. Walk around or do something entirely different to relieve the tension that builds up. Cutting puzzle pieces requires you to sit perfectly still and concentrate on cutting the perfect jigsaw puzzle piece each time. After a while stiffness will develop in your neck and back. It's gradual and insidious. Pace yourself.

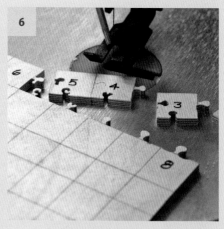

8 Cut the third row. Don't rush the process of cutting pieces. Smooth cuts are what give wooden jigsaw puzzle pieces that delightful feel in the fingers. Note that there are several fancy knobs sprinkled among the knobs.

9 Begin the last two rows. On a strip cut, the last two rows should be cut together. By doing this, you will end with four pieces to cut and have more wood to hold onto under the foot of the machine. Reduce the rpm on the machine to below 500. This will slow the blade and improve control, allowing you to move the piece through the blade precisely.

10 Cut the last four pieces. Since these last four pieces are 1" (25mm) squares, you probably will not need a pusher stick. Make your cuts slow and smooth.

PUZZLE ONE: Strip Cutting *(continued)*

11 **Vacuum the pieces.** Pour the finished pieces into the sieve and vacuum off the sawdust.

12 **Assemble and store.** You never get all the sawdust off of a newly finished puzzle until it has been assembled at least once—so go ahead and assemble it. After all, assembling a freshly cut wooden jigsaw puzzle you've just made is fun and the relaxing part of the exercise! Store the pieces in a container afterward.

PUZZLE 2: SECTIONING A PUZZLE BLANK

No matter which method you use to cut puzzle pieces, you must get the puzzle blank to a manageable size. The larger the puzzle blank, the larger the arc needed to make the turns for cutting the interlocks and knobs. A small- to medium-size puzzle blank reduces the size of the arc and thus is easier to manipulate.

For this practice puzzle project, we will cut ⅝" (16mm) puzzle pieces. You will need the 5" x 7½" (127mm x 191mm) plywood puzzle blank. This puzzle blank is small enough and didn't

need to be sectioned, but we cut it in half for practice. Most large puzzles need to be sectioned to make them easier to manipulate when cutting small precise puzzle pieces.

Summary of steps:
1. Mark the centers of the edges.
2. Cut the first interlocks on the halfway mark.
3. Complete cutting the blank in half.
4. Cut into quarters if the blank is still too large.
5. Cut out the pieces.

PUZZLE TWO: Sectioning

1 **Stain the blank.** Select a nice oil- or water-based stain, dilute it, brush it on the nice side of the puzzle blank, and wipe it off.

2 **Finish the blank.** After 24 hours, draw pencil lines ⅝" (16mm) apart along each side to form a grid. Use a tack-rag on the piece to remove all sawdust. Apply an acrylic or lacquer spray, or brush on a light varnish finish.

3 **Cut the blank in half.** At the mid-point of the 7½" (191mm) side of the blank, begin cutting knobs and interlocks to section the blank in half. Cut in about ¼" (6mm) and make an interlock. Cut a little less than ½" (13mm) and cut another interlock. Cut a knob or interlock on the center of each square.

4 **Cut the first row.** On one-half of the puzzle blank, strip cut the first row. In the photo, you can see I cut five pieces, several with fancy knobs.

Tip: Spacing the Interlocks

The space between these interlocks will determine the size of your pieces. Therefore, the closer you make these interlocks, the smaller your pieces will be. Be careful not to make the interlock spacing so small that you cannot cut puzzle pieces between them.

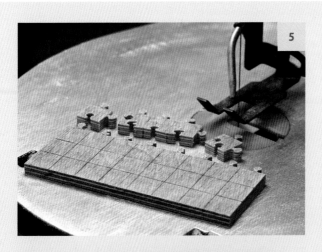

5 **Continue to strip cut the puzzle.** At ⅝" (16mm), the puzzle pieces are definitely smaller than the previous project and take a little more time and concentration to cut perfectly. If you feel that 800 rpm is too fast, reduce the blade speed to a more comfortable feed rate.

6 **Cut some faux edge pieces.** Note how straight the lines are cut. When you make these in a picture puzzle, look for coloring similar to the actual edge pieces. The closer they resemble the real edge pieces, the more difficult they will be to assemble.

7 **Cut the last rows.** As we did in the first project, cut the last two rows together. It gives more stability as you work closer and closer under the foot of the scroll saw.

PUZZLE TWO: Sectioning *(continued)*

8 **Cut the last pieces.**
Keep the blade speed below
500 rpm. Cutting these small
pieces needs to be done
slowly, with a light touch,
to assure no mistakes.

9 **Vacuum the pieces.**
Finished at last! Pour the
jigsaw puzzle pieces into
the sieve and vacuum the
sawdust from them.

10 **Assemble.** A puzzle
is not really complete until
it's been used and enjoyed.
Putting a just-finished
wooden jigsaw puzzle
together is part of the fun
of making the puzzle in the
first place.

PUZZLE 3: STAIR-STEP CUTTING

Using the strip-cutting method free-hand without guidelines can result in a situation upon arriving at the last row. The row can either be too big, resulting in puzzle pieces larger than the rest; or the row can be too small, resulting in tiny puzzle pieces. Large pieces are not a problem to cut, but making tiny puzzle pieces can often result in cutting errors. One way to avoid this mishap is to use the stair-step method.

This last blank practice puzzle is difficult and small. For this project, you will be cutting ½" (13mm)-sized pieces.

You will find that pieces of this size impart little information to the assembler and create a difficult puzzle. The trick to making such small pieces is to use a light touch on the work and to feed the plywood blank slowly.

Summary of steps:

1. Cut the first piece on a corner.
2. Cut the next piece beside the first as if you are strip-cutting. Now cut the piece directly below the corner piece. These three pieces begin the stair-step.
3. Continue cutting in a stair-step pattern across the blank.

PUZZLE THREE: Stair-Step Cutting

1 Prepare the blank.
Apply a diluted light stain to a 5" x 7" (127mm x 178mm) blank. Let the blank dry overnight. Use a square to draw pencil lines ½" (13mm) apart along each side to form a grid. Apply a finish and let it dry overnight.

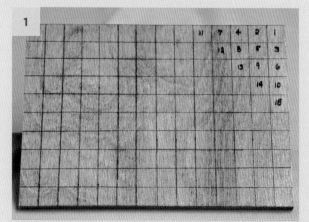

2 Cut the first piece.
Starting from the right corner, cut out piece marked number one as shown. The numbers on the grid are for illustration only. You need not write them in the squares of your practice puzzle blank.

3 Cut the first stair step.
Cut pieces numbered two and three. Be patient and cut slowly and carefully, making gentle curves. Use a slower rpm, such as 600. Take care to leave enough wood through the neck of each knob.

4 Cut the second and third steps. It's early in the project to think about taking a break, but deciding when to do something else should be in your mind as you cut the stair-step pieces. Continue to cut puzzle pieces four through ten.

5 Cut some fancy knobs. Making fancy knobs on ½" (13mm) pieces is demanding, but not impossible. Carefully plan the cuts, use a light pressure, and slow the scroll saw blade speed to below 500. Continue cutting.

6 Cut the last few pairs. Remember, when you get to the last six or eight pieces, cut them together in pairs. The last four pieces will end up under the foot of the machine (if you choose to keep the foot on) and are tedious to maneuver. Reduce the blade speed to below 500 rpm and use a wood guide to hold the piece steady. Cut smoothly and slowly.

7 Complete the puzzle. Congratulations! You've completed a 140-piece puzzle. Vacuum off the sawdust using your sieve and place the finished puzzle in its box.

Three project puzzle pieces and a quarter.

Progress

Congratulations on your progress so far. Making a wooden jigsaw puzzle without a picture is designed to allow you to concentrate on the shape of the puzzle piece and how it is made. So far you've successfully completed three puzzles with smaller and smaller jigsaw puzzle pieces. You have strip-cut and stair-step cut pieces, and made fancy knobs, faux edges, and interlocks. You sectioned a puzzle blank. All of these projects have hopefully provided you with experience and confidence that you can cut smaller and smaller jigsaw puzzle pieces. The photo above shows the three sizes you have cut in relation to a quarter. It's now time to move to practice jigsaw puzzles with images. In the following pages, you'll make two practice jigsaw puzzles that will also become difficult and challenging puzzles when they are completed.

PUZZLE 4: SMALL FREEHAND STYLE

Freehand cutting is creative and allows for a variety in the shapes of pieces. The puzzle maker still cuts each piece more or less in a row down or across the puzzle blank. However, because the cuts are made without guides or marks, each piece is unique. The resulting freehand pieces are never quite the same shape and are interesting to look at when assembling the puzzle.

Cutting small precise wooden puzzle pieces freehand is what makes these puzzles both fascinating and difficult at the same time. This project will concentrate on the steps necessary to prepare a plywood board to receive a digital photo and how to exactly cut small puzzle pieces from this puzzle blank. Reread the section on photo paper on page 19 if you need a refresher.

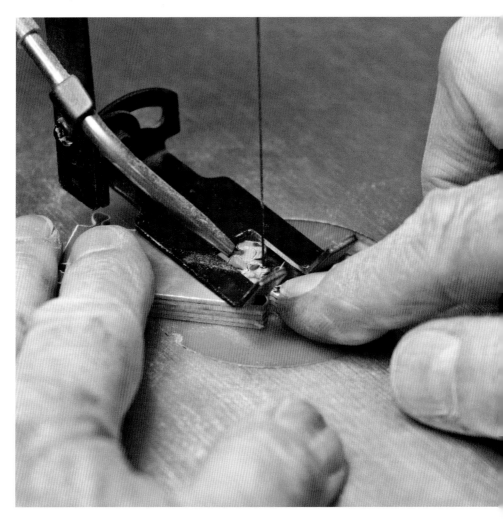

PUZZLE FOUR: Small Freehand Style

1 Prepare the blank. Use a vacuum and then a tack-rag to remove all sawdust from the face of the plywood board.

2 Apply spray adhesive. Use painter's tape to temporarily hold the image to the paper so it doesn't move when you spray. Place both the photo and the plywood board on a clean sheet of paper. At the distance indicated on the spray can label, apply a very light coat of adhesive on both surfaces. Take care not to over coat the surfaces.

3 Attach the image to the blank. After spraying both surfaces, wait the prescribed time for a double bond and carefully place the photo on the plywood board. Begin at one corner and slowly lay the photo down onto the plywood, working from one side to the other. Once the photo is down on the plywood, use a clean roller to assure there are no bubbles remaining between the surfaces and the bond is solid throughout.

4 Allow the puzzle blank to cure. It takes the adhesive about 24 hours to fully set. The instructions on the can may tell you that you can use the glued piece earlier than that, but they usually mean adhering photos to cardboard or other material that isn't going to be cut into small puzzle pieces. As in most woodworking projects, wait the 24 hours to let the piece dry thoroughly.

5 Draw a guideline. When the time has elapsed for the adhesive to fully set, draw a guideline down the center of the 7" (178mm) side of the puzzle blank.

6 Section the puzzle. Obviously, we could cut this small puzzle without sectioning, but this is good practice. Begin by cutting down the pencil line about ¼" (6mm) and make a knob.

5

7 Continue sectioning. Continue to cut. Produce another knob a little less than ½" (13mm) down the line from the first knob. Note the fancy knob in the second position. Stay with the faint pencil line and make knobs about ½" (13mm) apart down the center of the blank. Make sure that the last knob is at least ¼" (6mm) from the edge of the blank.

8 Complete sectioning. You have divided the puzzle blank into two pieces, 2½" x 3½" (64mm x 89mm) with knobs on one side of each piece. The picture used as the example for this project is one I took of the annual Chincoteague pony drive on Assateague Island, Virginia.

9 Begin strip cutting. The first half of the puzzle will be strip cut. Begin cutting jigsaw puzzle pieces at one corner. It's easiest to select the edge with the knobs.

PUZZLE FOUR: Small Freehand Style *(continued)*

10 Carry on strip cutting. If you can, make a fancy knob along the way. Try to keep the pieces about ½" (13mm) square. This is about the smallest size that provides the flexibility to make good knobs and even a fancy one every once in a while.

11 Continue cutting. Lower the rpm to below 500. The scroll saw blade is moving slower and we can feed the piece slowly through the blade to make the cuts.

12 Cut the last two rows. Always leave a double row of six or eight pieces to cut at the end of a puzzle section. This provides a larger piece of the puzzle blank to hold onto under the foot of the machine. Take your time and cut slowly and evenly. Pause if necessary to see where you are going with the blade.

Tip: Take a Break

Just a reminder: fatigue invites mistakes. The concentration required for cutting precise puzzle pieces gradually induces tiredness. Sometimes it's not really noticeable, so the only way to combat this problem is to make it a routine to take a break each 30-45 minutes.

13 Cut the last pieces in the first half. With the rpm still below 500, cut the last two pieces for the first half of the puzzle. The entire piece is now under the foot, so the procedure to make this last cut is slow and easy. The foot of the machine shouldn't be adjusted to press too tightly against the work, as it will make it hard to move through the blade. Conversely, too loose a foot pressure and the small piece will jump up and down. You can control this somewhat with a wooden guide.

14 Begin cutting the second half. For the other section, use the stair-step cut. This method allows you to estimate the number of rows you can easily freehand cut from this section. In the photo, you can see that the ruler shows there is about $7/8$" (22mm) remaining. This will be tight, but two rows can be cut from that part of the blank.

Tip: Plan the Interlocks

Be conscious of where the interlocks will be and preplan the cuts before you make them. After you cut the first interlock, look at how far it extends into the piece, and start the interlock on the other side of the piece a little off center. When the top of the interlock is cut, there will be enough wood left to have a strong puzzle piece.

PUZZLE FOUR: Small Freehand Style *(continued)*

15 Finish the puzzle. When nearing the last pieces to be cut from a puzzle, there is a growing sense of accomplishment. But still there are five pieces to cut, and now is not the time to relax. Reduce the rpm, make the cuts gradually, and ease the work through the blade. Make gentle, smooth curves that feel as good as they look.

15

16 Clean up the pieces. On your breaks, you probably selected a box to house this puzzle project and noted a name in advance. When the last pieces are cut, pour them into the sieve and vacuum off the sawdust.

17 Assemble. Carefully transfer the pieces to the box. Take the new puzzle to a table and spread it out for the first assembly. It's exciting to turn over the newly cut pieces and see how they look all spread out. Then the fun and delight of assembly begins.

17

In my version of this finished puzzle, note that the opposite corners have been cut to resemble interior pieces. On the interior there are four pieces that resemble exterior edge pieces. This 5" x 7" (127mm x 178mm) puzzle contains 174 pieces, and usually takes three to four enjoyable hours to assemble. All will enjoy a happy and a relaxing afternoon every time it is put together. And yet, you say to yourself, it was just a practice project. But it's also a useful and now a valued jigsaw puzzle.

Note that a puzzle piece design has been painted on the top of the puzzle box. This is the symbol that I use to designate this box contains a jigsaw puzzle I have made. You may want to decorate your puzzle boxes with your own identifying symbol.

PUZZLE 5: LARGE FREEHAND STYLE

For the final project in this chapter, we
will use the 8" x 10" (203mm x 254mm)
puzzle board and digital photo you've
chosen to use. I chose a shot of my two
kittens when they were just six weeks old.

PUZZLE FIVE: Large Freehand Style

1 **Prepare to adhere the digital photograph to the puzzle blank.** Place the plywood puzzle blank on a clean piece of butcher paper or newspaper on a flat surface and put the photo face down next to it. Don't forget to use the ring of painter's tape to secure the image while you are spraying the back with adhesive. Carefully vacuum off any sawdust from the plywood. Now take the tack-rag and remove the rest of the dust. Shake the spray adhesive bottle vigorously and apply a light coat of adhesive on both surfaces.

2 **Attach the photo to the blank.** Wait the prescribed amount of time for the adhesive to dry to a tacky state. Place the photo on the plywood blank at one corner.

3 **Smooth the image.** When you place the image on the blank, use the roller to smooth out the image and assure yourself there are no bubbles left between the two surfaces.

4 **Draw guidelines.** Use a square to draw a light pencil line down the center of the 10" (254mm) side. Draw a second intersecting pencil line down the center of the 8" (203mm) side. These two lines are your guidelines for cutting the puzzle into segments.

5 **Cut the puzzle blank in half.** This will reduce the size of the puzzle blank sections and make them more manageable. Begin on the 10" (254mm) side and cut interlocks and knobs about ½" (13mm) or less apart freehand along the pencil line. Remember to start ¼" (6mm) in from the edge with your first interlock.

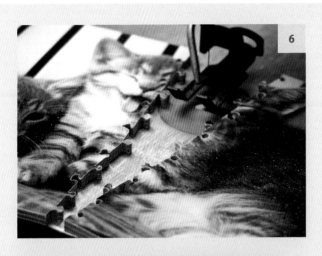

6 Complete cutting the puzzle in half. Continue cutting along the guideline making knobs, both fancy and rounded, as you go. Watch the spacing of the knobs, as this will determine how many pieces you can cut along that edge of the puzzle blank. Make sure that the last knob is about a ¼" (6mm) from the edge of the puzzle blank.

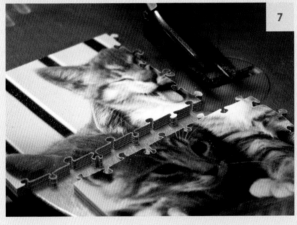

7 Cut the puzzle in quarters. Find the centerline for one of these segments. Cut in about ¼" (6mm), make a knob, and begin to divide this segment in half again. As before, keep the knobs a little less than ½" (13mm) apart center to center. Don't worry if you don't keep to the line or if you make the knobs more than a half-inch apart. Remember, you are cutting a puzzle freehand and you're allowed to wander around.

Tip: Change Blades

At this point, as we begin to cut a large puzzle, it's a good time to discuss when to change blades. Remember, new blades always cut cleaner and quicker than those that you have used for cutting fifty pieces. And blades that have cut a hundred or so pieces can be quite dull. It's a good practice to begin each session with a fresh blade. Cut about 75 to 100 pieces, less if you really want crisp cuts on all your puzzle pieces, and then replace the blade. When the blade is replaced, remember to reduce your blade speed to 550 to 600 rpm to take into account that this new blade will cut through the puzzle blank much quicker.

PUZZLE FIVE: Large Freehand Style *(continued)*

8 **Cut the second half in half.** Cut knobs and interlocks down the centerline on the other half of the puzzle blank. Once this process is complete, you will have sectioned the puzzle blank into four quarters. Now each of these segments will be easier to handle as you begin to cut puzzle pieces.

9 **Start cutting the first quarter.** Select a quarter section of the puzzle blank and start to make puzzle pieces on the side with the newly cut interlocks. Strip cut across a side of the blank using the interlocks as the spacing for cutting the pieces.

10 **Finish up this quarter.** As you near the last six or so pieces, slow the blade speed to about 450 rpm so you can hold onto the small blank under the foot of the machine and slowly cut the last four pieces. It is a delicate process to cut these last four puzzle pieces, so take your time and be precise.

11 **Stair-step cut the next quarter.**

12 **Prepare to insert a fancy figure.** Because my puzzle uses a cat photograph, I'm using a cat figure, but use a figure that is appropriate for your puzzle subject. First, determine about where the figure should be placed. Stair-step cut enough pieces to reach the location.

13

13 **Trace the figure.** Place the puzzle blank face down and put the figure in the proper orientation on the blank. Make a pencil outline of the figure on the back of the puzzle blank so a part of the figure is adjacent to the edge of the stair step.

14

14 **Cut out the figure.** With the puzzle blank face down, cut out the figure. The reverse tooth blade cuts smoothly in both directions, so there won't be tear-out from cutting this way. If the parts of your figure are delicate, use a blade speed of about 550-600 rpm. The photo at left shows the cat cut away from the puzzle blank. As you can see, the entrance cut was made into the cat figure at the corner of the middle stair step.

Tip: Losing a Row

In the photo at right, you can see the five strips I cut and re-assembled. Note the seven fancy knobs in this group of puzzle pieces. Most of these pieces look like each other and are harder to assemble. The group of assembled puzzle pieces is a good example of freehand cutting as

it shows that there is a variation in the size and shape of puzzle pieces. On the left side there are five rows, but on the other side there are only four. One row has been lost. The sectioning was not exactly straight, and I had to compensate by reducing the rows by one. A close inspection of the puzzle pieces inside this set shows that some bigger pieces were cut in half to make the full five rows and restore the balance.

PUZZLE FIVE: Large Freehand Style *(continued)*

15 **Cut the figure into more pieces.** Turn the puzzle blank and the figure right side up. Since the cat figure is quite large, I will cut it into puzzle pieces to disguise it. Note in the photo at right that the corner has two interlocks cut in it. When the last piece is cut, the corner piece will resemble an interior piece. We continue to cut puzzle pieces on the stair step.

16 **Finish up this section.** Reduce the blade speed to cut the last six or eight pieces. After the last pieces are placed in the bowl, it's a natural place to take a break. Change blades.

17 **Start the third section.** Take the third quarter of the puzzle blank, reduce the rpm on your machine to accommodate the new blade, and cut the puzzle pieces in a stair-step fashion.

18 **Continue cutting.** We need to hide this corner, so let's cut the corner on a diagonal and make two pieces. The photo at right shows two things. First, I've cut the corner into two interlocked diagonal pieces. Second, the puzzle piece next to it was too large, so I cut it into two pieces. The top one now resembles an edge piece. In freehand cutting, you'll sometimes find that you're cutting larger and larger pieces. This relates back to the spacing of our initial sectioning cuts. When this happens, the large pieces can be cut into two smaller pieces either cut on the diagonal or straight across, with another knob and interlock inserted if space will allow.

19 **Continue cutting stair-step style.** You can see that the rows are getting larger toward the bottom edge of the puzzle blank. As I cut these last pieces, I will try to make an extra row or two to reduce the size of the pieces.

20 Dealing with a piece that's too large.

The last few pieces of this last quarter of the puzzle turned out to be larger than I wanted. The best way to solve this is to cut it in half. This puzzle piece was cut partially on the diagonal with an interlock to make two smaller pieces. One is, as you can see, a faux edge piece.

21 Complete cutting.

The last part of this puzzle blank was supposed to be cut into four large pieces. Instead, they were cut into six pieces. The corner piece is cut to resemble an interior piece like the one on the opposite corner of the puzzle. Note how the two large pieces were divided into four puzzle pieces. The corner piece, because of the two false interlocks, was not suitable to cut in half, nor was the puzzle piece next to the corner.

22 Vacuum the pieces.

What a beautiful pile of puzzle pieces! Pour the 335 pieces into the sieve and vacuum the sawdust off of them. When you're satisfied you've gotten enough dust off, transfer the pieces to the box or container you've designated for this puzzle. With the puzzle in its proper home, take it from the shop into the house and find a place to spread it out.

This completes the five practice jigsaw puzzle projects. If you have diligently made each practice puzzle, you have cut more than 700 individual jigsaw puzzle pieces. You know how to use both contact cement and spray adhesive to adhere images to jigsaw puzzle blanks. You have learned how to make fancy figure blanks, and have inserted at least one fancy figure cutout and made it part of a jigsaw puzzle. This practice provided you with the skill and experience to craft difficult one-of-a-kind wooden heirloom jigsaw puzzles. As you can attest, each wooden jigsaw puzzle that is cut out freehand is unique. It is truly a custom product and will be treasured by anyone lucky enough to receive one. Congratulations on your accomplishment!

CHAPTER 3

Step-by-Step Projects

Though you have crafted five practice puzzles in the

previous chapter, this will be the first of the larger puzzles

you'll construct. That's an exciting prospect! So let's begin

the project. Select a pre-made puzzle blank or make a

new one using the instructions on page 26–27. I suggest

making a blank about 8½" by 11" (216mm by 279mm).

This is a nice measurement for a full-size wooden jigsaw

puzzle. It will result in about 400 to 450 pieces and

present quite a degree of difficulty to assemble.

This last project will
walk you through
the creation of
your first full-size
heirloom puzzle.

JIGSAW PUZZLE: Step-by-Step

1 Choose the puzzle blank. Choose a puzzle blank that offers a real quandary for the assembler. Once cut into small puzzle pieces, a picture with repeating shapes and colors will be quite confusing. The image I selected for my puzzle is called "Savannah Lilies." It is a photo I took on a visit to the harbor at Savannah, Georgia a few years ago.

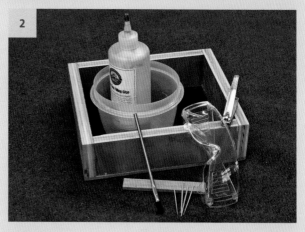

2 Assemble the equipment. Once you've chosen the puzzle blank, it's time to assemble the equipment for the project: the sieve, a bowl for collecting the puzzle pieces, wood glue, toothpicks, toenail clippers, a ¼" (6mm) brush, a short ³⁄₁₆" (5mm)-thick piece of wood to use as a guide, and a pair of safety glasses.

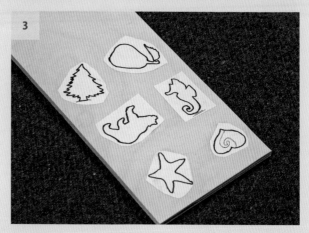

3 Plan the puzzle. The next step in the process is planning the puzzle. Because the puzzle blank is large, it should be sectioned in four pieces. Also, plan some fancy figures to hide in the puzzle. Perhaps you could use a tricky kind of cut in one or two places. You should note all of these items on a pad or notebook for future reference.

4 Select the fancy figures. Here are some fancy figures I like. I'll select three for my puzzle blank. An uneven number of fancy figures are appropriate for a puzzle of this size, and when placed at strategic spots within the puzzle, they will add diversity and interest for the assembler.

5 Cut the puzzle blank in half. Draw a small pencil mark in the center of the long side as a reference. Cut the knobs and interlocks a little less than ½" (13mm) apart. With this spacing between interlocks, you will be able to make nice ½" (13mm) square jigsaw puzzle pieces. Cut some fancy interlocks as you go. Remember, so that you don't give the assembler a "gift," to cut more than one interlock that has the same shape.

6 Cut the halves in half. Cut the two halves in half again. Mark the center of the edge as a guide. When complete, you'll have four easy-to-handle blanks each measuring about 4¼" x 5½" (108mm x 140mm). Another benefit of cutting a puzzle blank into smaller sections is that the knob and interlock spacing sets up the section for cutting puzzle pieces.

JIGSAW PUZZLE: Step-by-Step *(continued)*

7 Complete planning of the puzzle. Divide a page of your notebook into four sections that correspond to the puzzle. Number 1 to 4, starting at top left going clockwise. Make a complete plan for the puzzle: hide corners, place figures, etc. In my example, most of the pieces will be small and square. I'm also going to cut two areas using a method I call "ocean wave" (see sidebar on page 73).

8 Start section #1. Begin with section #1. Start cutting at the inside corner where the two sets of knobs meet. Use a stair-step cut to set up the lines of pieces.

Remember to Change the Blade

When is a good time to change saw blades? The obvious quick answer is when the blade is dull. But how do you know when a blade is dull and needs changing? You see fuzzy edges on the puzzle pieces, you say. Well, do we want to wait until we have a really dull blade? Usually waiting that long isn't a good practice if you want to make crisp-looking puzzle pieces all the time. A good procedure is to begin each cutting session with a new blade. Cut about 60 to 75 or so pieces, then carefully examine the last few. If, under the magnifying glass, you see slightly ragged paper edges, change the blade. It's always better to change the blade earlier than later. Remember, a new blade will always cut faster, so reduce the speed to about 600 rpm.

The Ocean Wave Cut

The ocean wave cut uses a curvy cut to create interlocks that look like waves. I typically start on a corner. There are many ways to organize wave cuts together. I like to have the wave cuts spread out from a corner, morphing gradually into square puzzle pieces. Aim to get back to square pieces within about 3" or 4" (76mm or 102mm) square from the corner.

Practice on the corners of a small piece of puzzle board. Remember, the idea is to make a corner area using the ocean wave cut, and then carefully make knobs and interlocks to line up with the other part of the puzzle. Take your time and make graceful curves in the cutting of these pieces. Don't be too concerned about how large the pieces become. Concentrate on smooth, wavelike curves. When the pieces are placed unassembled on a surface, they look quite unusual. Finding mates for these appealing curved pieces can defy assembly. Practice cutting with this technique until you feel comfortable with it.

This practice board shows puzzle pieces cut using the ocean wave technique.

Unassembled ocean wave puzzle pieces.

JIGSAW PUZZLE: Step-by-Step *(continued)*

9 **Cut the corner of section #1.** When you have enough confidence in your ability to make graceful ocean wave puzzle pieces (see sidebar on page 73), cut artful curved pieces from the corner of section #1 using the method. Cut the puzzle pieces slowly and gracefully. Try to align the knob and interlocks with those of the rest of the puzzle blank.

10 **Cut the rest of section #1.** When the ocean wave corner is complete, it is time to finish cutting the rest of the section. Strip cut adjacent to the ocean wave section to even out the rows. Next, use the stair-step cut to bring the two corner sections into alignment. Continue cutting pieces and complete section #1.

11 **Begin section #2.** Begin section #2 by using the stair-step method to get into a position to place the first fancy figure. You should also cut some faux interlocks into the corner piece. For my fancy figure, I chose the butterfly template. Locate your template next to the stair step in a central part of the section.

12 Trace the figure.

Turn the puzzle blank over and situate the template in the chosen position. With a pencil, draw a line around the template. Note the orientation of the template is still toward the top of the blank and is in the position we chose when the image was showing.

13 Cut the figure.

With the back of the puzzle blank facing up, cut around the figure outline. Because you are using a reverse skip tooth blade, the blade will cut cleanly without causing tearout on the image side. To hide the figure, cut it into several pieces. Cut pieces around the figure using the stair step.

14 Place a second figure.

Keep cutting until you get to a point where you want to place a second template. The heart figure I chose is quite small, so I'll do something a bit different when I cut it out. Turn the puzzle blank face down and draw a pencil outline of the template.

JIGSAW PUZZLE: Step-by-Step *(continued)*

15 Cut the small figure.

The way to handle a small figure template is to cut it into puzzle pieces while it is still connected to the blank. If I cut the heart from the blank, it would be too small to hold under the foot of the saw and could result in a miss-cut. The best way to make two puzzle pieces out of such a small figure is to cut it while it's part of the blank.

16 Cut faux edge pieces.

Turn the puzzle blank face up. Try to cut a pair of faux edge pieces into each section of the puzzle. The edge should be cut exactly straight and smooth to make it resemble a real edge piece. Make sure the colors are similar to some part of the real edge.

17 Complete section #2.

Reduce the scroll saw rpm as your puzzle blank gets smaller. Especially when cutting the last few pieces of the section, it is critical to take time and not rush. Use a guide stick as you cut the last few pieces under the foot of the machine.

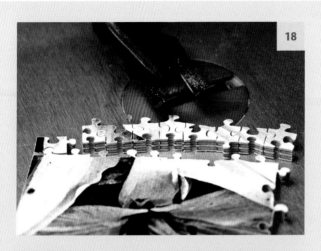

18 Begin section #3. To do something different, strip cut a row of puzzle pieces. Be sure to add a few fancy knobs for interest. Let's plan to cut the corner using the ocean wave method.

19 Make stair-step cuts. Next, switch to a stair step cut for several rows. This begins to set the rows of puzzle pieces. Also, when you cut the ocean wave pieces, you'll be able to better estimate where to cut the connecting knobs.

20 Begin the ocean wave corner. It takes more time and greater concentration to cut curved ocean wave pieces. Don't be concerned if the pieces are larger than the little square ones you've been cutting. It will be just fine. The wave pieces are interesting to look at and present a different spatial problem for the assembler.

Take a break!

Remember to rest your eyes every 30-45 minutes to stay your sharpest.

JIGSAW PUZZLE: Step-by-Step *(continued)*

21 Complete the ocean wave cut. Carefully estimate where the connecting knobs will be placed and cut them. Remember, you're transitioning into straight lines and square pieces as you go away from the corner. Don't forget to throw in a faux edge piece or two.

22 Continue cutting section #3. The interlocks should line up fairly well, and you can cut another faux edge piece, too. Strip cut along the straight edge of the blank and work toward the main part of the blank. This will even up the rows to allow us to complete this section.

23 Cut some trick pieces. When I reached the main part of the puzzle blank section, I cut a double interlock puzzle piece due to size restrictions. Try it out! It makes a nice-looking faux edge puzzle piece. Continue the strip cut into the rest of section #3.

24 Complete section #3.
Using the wood guide stick and a slow blade speed of about 475 rpm, cut the last four pieces of this section. When the rpm is slowed, the small puzzle blank area doesn't tend to jump up and down as much and can be controlled more easily. The wood guide steadies the puzzle blank so the piece can be cut easily.

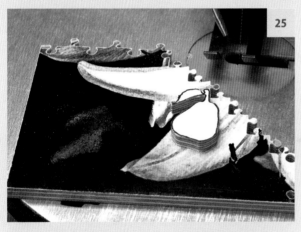

25 Begin section #4.
This section will have a fancy figure (I chose a pear) inserted in a good spot on the puzzle blank. Cut stair-step style to about the middle of the blank. Place the figure template facing upward on the blank.

26 Cut the figure from the blank. As you've done before with the other fancy figure templates, turn the puzzle blank over, reposition the template, and draw a pencil line around it. With the puzzle blank still face down, cut around the figure.

JIGSAW PUZZLE: Step-by-Step *(continued)*

27 **Cut the figure into pieces.** Turn over the puzzle blank and cut the figure into five or so puzzle pieces. Continue to cut the stair step through the area where the figure shape was removed.

28 **Cut trick pieces.** In my puzzle, the dark portion of the puzzle blank is an ideal spot to make another pair of faux edge pieces. These pieces are the same color as the real edge pieces. Just make the edge cut absolutely straight.

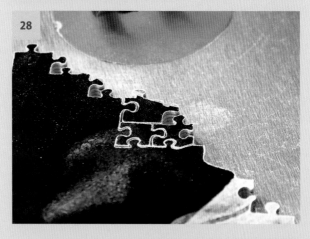

29 **Continue the stair-step cut.** Cut the stair step toward the corner of the section. As you get closer to the end, try not to cut too quickly. When the end of a project is in sight, we sometimes start to rush, and that's how mistakes are made. Reduce the rpm and slow down to assure each piece is cut precisely.

30 Complete the puzzle.

To hide this corner, make a cut just past the corner and then cut diagonally. Other pieces were treated the same way to cause the assembler to pause when trying to find these pieces. If possible, always make more than one of a special kind of puzzle piece. This adds a level of adversity to the assembly.

31 Clean up the pieces.

It is a satisfying moment to have all the jigsaw puzzle pieces in the bowl. Take a moment to look at all those pieces you've cut precisely and without error. Pour the puzzle pieces into the sieve and run the vacuum over the bottom. Shake the pieces gently, and try to get as much of the sawdust off as possible.

32 Assemble the puzzle.

It's time to see how this jigsaw puzzle turned out. Spread out the new jigsaw puzzle on a table and begin assembly. Hopefully, it's as difficult and interesting as you believed. In my version, the 504 jigsaw pieces were small enough to not give up many clues as to where they mated with each other.

BOXING YOUR PUZZLE

Once a jigsaw puzzle has been cut into individual puzzle pieces, what's next? You've got to put it somewhere. OK, you could put the pieces in a paper bag or a zip-lock plastic bag. They're both containers, are they not? The bags would serve the purpose of holding all those beautifully cut little jigsaw puzzle pieces, wouldn't they? Perhaps. But, then, would you really want to show off an heirloom wooden jigsaw puzzle in a plastic bag? Probably that's not in your plan. You've put many hours of time into carefully making this heirloom puzzle. It needs an attractive box to compliment the intricately cut jigsaw puzzle housed within.

Choosing a box

Here are some questions you may want to consider in deciding on a box or container for your jigsaw puzzle. What's the destination of this jigsaw puzzle? Will it be a gift, or will this puzzle be added to your own personal collection? Do you plan to sell this puzzle? The answers to these questions should provide a framework for the kind of box or container you plan to use.

Many times, if I've not decided on a destination for a jigsaw puzzle I am making, I put the finished puzzle in a plastic food container for safekeeping. Later, when I know what I will do with the puzzle, I transfer it to a

There are a wide variety of boxes that are suitable for containing puzzles.

This stationary box holds the practice puzzle from pages 56–60.

specially constructed box that fits the puzzle's destination. At other times, the destination presents itself while I am crafting the jigsaw puzzle and I construct the box as a diversion to cutting pieces.

Grocery stores have quite a variety of plastic food containers that are attractive and useful. The lids stay tight and are usually brightly colored. Choosing clear plastic containers will show off your intricately cut jigsaw puzzle pieces quite nicely and give a utilitarian look to the work.

Specialty stationary stores are another excellent source for more attractive ready-made boxes. These stores usually have pasteboard boxes covered with decorative paper. Some shops carry brightly colored nesting boxes. Sometimes there can be as many as four, five or even six boxes in a nest. If a box nest is the right size, each box in the nest can be employed as a lovely puzzle box. The nice part of using these boxes is that no finishing work is involved other than making the label or perhaps painting your identifying mark on the lid. Such a box feels good in the hands and makes an attractive puzzle box to keep or to give as a gift.

Craft stores carry a variety of finished and unfinished boxes. Many come in an array of fun shapes. Some unfinished boxes resemble books, while others are in the shapes of octagons, stars, rectangles, or circles, to name a few.

This octagonal box from a craft store was a good puzzle box choice.

The octagonal box pictured above was purchased at a craft outlet store. The resources in a craft store are almost endless. Some of the boxes will be made of cardboard covered with paper, while others will be made of a soft wood, such as pine. Some of these boxes are unfinished and will need to be finished in some way. Others will be finished and ready to use, as was the brown chest we chose for the kitten puzzle on page 61.

To use an unfinished paper covered box from a craft store, it will be necessary to seal the box first to keep it from warping when it is painted.

Usually spraying lacquer or brushing on a penetrating wood finish or shellac will provide a seal coat. Once the box is coated with a sealer inside and out, it can be finished with either oil or water based paint.

Your woodshop, if you are a woodworker with a number of power tools, is another great box-building resource. You can build a high quality wooden box. This option is the best for really special gift containers or sales pieces. A handmade wooden box with finger or dovetail joints on the corners and a sliding or hinged lid with a distinctive metal catch makes a beautiful presentation vehicle for an heirloom jigsaw puzzle. Another nice touch is adding a beautiful colored velvet bag with a colorful drawstring.

Unexpected sources can yield useful puzzle boxes. One year, when my wife was baking cookies for Christmas, I came looking around for a box for my latest jigsaw puzzle. I had discovered I was one gift box short. As I stood in the kitchen smelling all the wonderful baked cookie odors coming from the oven, I glanced at the brightly colored round metal containers she was using to store her confections and got an idea. My wife, as it turned out, had an extra container. So I selected one of these round metal containers with a wonderful old time Christmas scene in full color on the lid for my last puzzle box. I used a spare red Christmas paper napkin to line the tin, and put the puzzle in a plastic bag so it wouldn't shake and give away what was inside the tin. I put the tin in a nice gift box and wrapped it as a Christmas present. It worked out perfectly. Keep your eyes open—you never know where you'll see a potential puzzle box!

Labeling your puzzle

This may sound self-explanatory or trivial, but labeling is an important part of the puzzle-making process. If you don't include a picture of the puzzle, then the label can give a hint as to what the puzzle may be about or what it may depict. Labels should contain four pieces of information:

1. The name of the puzzle.
2. The number of puzzle pieces.
3. The name of the maker.
4. The month and year the puzzle was made.

If you wish, the size of the puzzle can be included as well. The label can be placed on the top of the container, on the side, or on the inside. When the label is placed on the side, the puzzle box can be stored on a shelf with the label showing. If you use a handmade wooden box, the label can be affixed to the inside of the lid or placed on an inner side of the box so as to preserve the finished outsides.

Include a picture or not?

Commercially made cardboard puzzles usually have pictures on the box. They help the assembler understand where the pieces may fit. This picture provides clues to solving the puzzle. Another reason the puzzle manufacturer puts a picture on the box is to entice you to buy this beautiful picture puzzle. You, too, can choose to provide a picture in the box of a wooden heirloom jigsaw puzzle you have crafted. You can take a picture of the puzzle blank before cutting. This image can be printed and placed in the puzzle box.

There is no real rule about whether or not to include a picture with a wooden jigsaw puzzle. Consider this: a jigsaw puzzle without a picture is definitely harder to assemble. It also adds an air of mystery as to what the image actually will be when the puzzle is finally finished.

If your goal is to make difficult but memorable jigsaw puzzles, then you may want to consider omitting a picture. Without a picture the puzzle assembler must carefully examine the puzzle pieces and try to fit them together based on color and shape.

Final thoughts

The satisfaction of completing a project is always a good feeling. Completing a hand-cut heirloom jigsaw puzzle provides the same sense of satisfaction but it goes one step further because it embodies something of the maker. The puzzle maker has spent many hours in precisely cutting out each jigsaw puzzle piece. The jigsaw puzzle becomes a kind of legacy for the maker. A wooden jigsaw puzzle is rugged and will live on through the years and give pleasure to those who attempt to assemble and reassemble it.

Not long ago, I found one of my father's hand-cut jigsaw puzzles and marveled at the intricate pieces he'd cut. I knew he'd cut this puzzle in

This finished wooden chest shows yet another option for puzzle boxes.

the early 1930s. Instead of a modern motorized variable speed scroll saw like the ones used today, I knew he cut his pieces on a Singer treadle sewing machine base he'd converted into a jigsaw. Because he only worked the treadle at about 90-120 rpm, I could see each saw mark on the edges of each piece. It was almost like seeing his fingers moving the puzzle blank through the saw.

My father's wooden jigsaw puzzle is a masterpiece of intricate complicated pieces. Though it only has 78 pieces, the way he cut the pieces ensured that it is quite tricky to put together. The simple pleasure in solving this heirloom jigsaw puzzle continues and it stands as his gift to us over the span of time. It's now a treasured family heirloom and his silent legacy.

The making of hand-cut wooden jigsaw puzzles is a true labor of love. It is quite demanding to craft such a project. Each piece must be preplanned in advance and cut perfectly without error. But when a jigsaw puzzle is finished and beautifully boxed, it is a wonderful lasting gift for anyone because it keeps on giving each time it's assembled.

A wooden jigsaw puzzle is a stress reliever. The assembler must concentrate on the pieces and their spatial relationships and forget the cares of everyday living for a brief time.

Puzzles also teach spatial recognition and logic to figure out where each piece fits. These wooden jigsaw puzzles will stand the test of time and provide many hours of enjoyment for friends and loved ones. They are a legacy the maker freely gives to those he loves. Take pleasure in the journey in providing a legacy for your family and friends to enjoy for years to come.

Appendix:
A Short History of Jigsaw Puzzles

The history of the wooden jigsaw puzzle is fascinating. By making heirloom puzzles, you are contributing to promoting a wonderful and a historic pastime. Learning about the early history of this endeavor gives us a sense of being part of a larger enterprise. But will reading about the history of jigsaw puzzles make you a better puzzle maker? It's entirely possible. You'll read here about ideas, techniques, and methods used by puzzle makers who have made wooden jigsaw puzzles in times past. It will give you some familiarity with the folks who made the first puzzles and why they did it.

The Beginning

The first thing to remember in reading a piece about the history of anything is that nothing happens in a vacuum. No matter what the specific piece of history you wish to read or discuss, that event occurred in the midst of, and as a result of, other happenings and discoveries that were ongoing at the time. The invention, if that's a good word, of wooden jigsaw puzzles began sometime in the 1750s or 1760s. Dates are uncertain. The first wooden jigsaw puzzles were developed either in England or in Europe, and researchers are unsure of this fact as well.

At the time these items were being used, they were not called "puzzles" at all. Instead, these collections of sawed up images were called "dissections." The word sounds more like a medical term for cutting up a frog, doesn't it? But that's the term that was first used to describe jigsaw puzzles.

OK, they weren't exactly jigsaw puzzles as we know them today. There were no small interlocking pieces, nor were there exciting pictures. These dissections were maps, cut up along country lines. They were used as geography learning aids for school children.

The students would lay all the pieces on a table and try to place one country piece against another to make a map. A disadvantage to this was if someone jarred the table, the pieces would slide apart from one another. To make a dissection, a printed map was glued on a thin mahogany, basswood, or other semi-hard wood board.

After the glue dried, the countries depicted on the map were colored different shades with watercolor paint.

Then someone would cut around each country to make a piece of the puzzle. The work was performed painstakingly by hand using a fret saw. Have you ever tried to make precise cuts by hand with a coping saw? If so, you understand what these early puzzle makers were up against.

The Fret Saw

Remember what I said in the beginning about events happening as a result of other events? Well, here is a perfect example. The people from the mid-seventeenth century who were making these dissections were using a very thin blade in a fret saw. Where did they get such a blade? And who developed such a saw for them to use anyway? Unfortunately, throughout most of history, before the patenting of inventions came into vogue, the names of inventors were not always recorded.

We do know that about a hundred years before these events, historians believe a German watchmaker figured out how to make a very thin fine-tooth blade from a clock spring. It seems he wanted to decorate his clocks by cutting decorative designs from very thin wood stock. This technique was called fretwork.

Before this time, fretwork was executed using a knife and a chisel. This clock maker figured it would be easier to use a very thin saw blade than a knife and

chisel. Clock springs were the finest steel to be had in those days. Of course, this thin steel spring was invented to replace pendulums that were used to drive the mechanisms in clocks.

In this history of wooden jigsaw puzzles, we won't go into steel making and the other associated inventions that lead to the invention, or development, of the clock spring. But you get the idea: everything builds on an invention or idea that was in use before.

So we have a European clock maker using a thin saw blade to cut intricate designs out of thin wood for clock cases. A little later, it's believed a French cabinetmaker named Boulle designed a U-shaped frame and a handle for the tiny saw blade so he could cut intricate shapes for inlaid and veneered furniture. As others began using this tool, the saw came to be called a "Buhl saw." Later, "Buhl saw" was dropped in favor of "fret saw."

More Dissections

Let's continue our story about wooden jigsaw puzzles. In about 1760, there was a London mapmaker by the name of John Spilsbury, who we know made dissected maps for the King. We know this because his name was printed on the back of the dissections he made. Also, he advertised that he made dissections in his literature. This mapmaker made dissections for schools as well. Historical literature tells us these items were still being used as teaching aids well into the 1800s.

Soon, many mapmakers and printers got into the business of making dissections of maps, of course, but also historical events and religious studies. Still, the dissections were aimed at educating children and not solely as a pastime.

The dissections were marketed to the wealthy, because working families had little money to spend on such expensive items. Keep this thought in mind, as this theme will be repeated.

In about 1870 or 1880, it's believed that the Milton Bradley Co. was the first to make a recreational puzzle for children. This item was called the "Smashed-Up Train," and it was quite popular. Other companies competed with Milton Bradley and made dissections of their own.

The Victorian Era

In the late 1800s, to broaden the audience for their dissections, puzzle makers turned to fiber board and cardboard as base materials. This move reduced the cost of producing puzzles. Cardboard boxes were also adopted, and this made puzzles affordable for the middle classes. At this time, most of the puzzle manufacturing was in the United States, but several firms in Europe also existed.

Something else was happening in the late 1800s. The Victorian era was invading the United States, as it had earlier in England. The Victorian era began when Queen Victoria was crowned Queen of England in 1837. Her reign lasted until 1901, but the Victorian era, as it was called, lasted somewhat longer. The Victorian era was a time of elaborate design and decorative changes in the architectural decoration of homes, furniture, and even office and industrial buildings. The emphasis was on adding graceful non-structural decoration to the structures. There were intricately curved brackets, corbels, finials, drops, spandrels, and running trim. It was expensive and time-consuming for a trim carpenter to hand cut these decorative items. As time passed, a definite need developed for a mechanical approach to making these trim pieces quickly and efficiently.

Soon, enterprising manufacturers designed a treadle-operated saw that operated a blade connected between a pair of arms. The treadle mechanism was adapted from a sewing machine. This machine, instead of moving a needle up and down, moved the saw blade using the same push rod and belt found in a sewing machine. A carpenter or furniture maker could now quickly cut up to three-inch-thick lumber with graceful curves. The manufacturers called this treadle-operated invention a scroll saw. It wasn't long until puzzle makers started using the machine.

All through this period, educational puzzles persisted. They were excellent teaching aids for young children. They taught shapes of items, encouraged hand-eye coordination, and exposed children to all sorts of knowledge that was printed on the puzzles. Slowly, however, some manufacturers began to use this educational tool for just plain fun.

During this period, several companies saw that if they could make puzzles cheaply enough, they could profit by the volume. However, around 1908, Parker Brothers still made puzzles by hand from thin wood board. Always looking for ways to stay ahead of their competition, the employees at Parker made puzzles more difficult by cutting on the color line.

Later, the Parker people began using thin saw blades in treadle jigsaws to create interlocking pieces. This clever method made puzzles stay together, rather than drift apart, if the table was jiggled or someone breathed on the puzzle.

In 1912, several hundred piece puzzles sold for about $5. This was a time when the average worker made just $50 a week. Clearly, these wooden jigsaw puzzles were too expensive for the average worker. The wealthy, however, delighted in these diversions. These jigsaw puzzles were bought and given as gifts by the upper classes. The wooden jigsaw puzzle became a favorite. Many, for whom cost wasn't important, would purchase a puzzle or two or three for entertainment at a weekend garden party. Guests would compete in teams to see who could complete their puzzle ahead of the other team.

The Depression

The interest in jigsaw puzzles peaked during the 1920s and 1930s, but was still a favorite pastime during the Depression years. Puzzles were manufactured out of cardboard and sold in brightly colored cardboard boxes with the picture of the puzzle on the front.

You'll recall I said in the introduction that my father made wooden jigsaw puzzles to rent out and earn money during the Depression. This happened all across the country during those hard times. A puzzle meant family enjoyment that didn't require going out to eat or buying a ticket to something. The whole family could participate in the activity, and it didn't require anything but a table, chairs, and a light over the table.

Manufactured cardboard puzzles were sold by the hundred thousand all across the country. During this time, there was a company called Par Puzzles that made wooden jigsaw puzzles. They were expensive, but the company did an excellent job marketing their puzzles to celebrities and the wealthy, who loved them. For a time during the Depression, Par Puzzles became the "Cadillac" of wooden jigsaw puzzles.

World War II

When the Depression was winding down, war clouds were brewing in Europe. World War II hit the U.S. when Pearl Harbor was attacked, and the country changed forever. Fathers went to war and wives went to the defense plant or volunteered to help the war effort.

A new pastime also was coming of age. An item called a radio was being sold, first as a high-priced luxury item, but soon it invaded every home. Over the evening meal, people would listen to the war news. On Sunday afternoons, people would gather around the radio to listen to music or a sports event. On weekdays, the radio's variety shows, afternoon soap operas, and popular music seeped in and took over as the most popular pastime. After the end of World War II, radio became a dominant force for information and diversion. Games and puzzles were still being played, but not to the extent they were in the 1920s and 1930s.

The Fifties

In the early 1950s, two major things happened. At Bell Labs, a group of scientists and engineers developed a thing called a transistor. And the engineers at General Electric improved a thing called the cathode ray tube. These two breakthroughs brought on the electronic age we know today. Batteries became smaller and smaller and so did transistors. Our pastimes changed from puzzles and board games to electronic recreation and communication.

Modern Times

Lately, however, things are changing again. Yes, we have computers, e-mail, cell phones, and television, but jigsaw puzzles, both wooden and cardboard, are still being sold.

A new high-end puzzle maker is now marketing wooden jigsaw puzzles. The company is Stave Puzzles, and as Par Puzzles did in the 1930s, they market their puzzles to those who can afford to buy a 250-piece puzzle for $495. Others have followed Stave, and are marketing their handmade wooden jigsaw puzzles on the Internet. Also, commercially manufactured puzzles are still a viable part of our recreational industry.

This book invites you to become a contributor to this enjoyable pastime. You have in your hands the techniques you need to craft your own wooden jigsaw puzzles for your family and friends. As many have found over the years, puzzles are a great stress reliever and a source of intense enjoyment. There are techniques and methods to making wooden jigsaw puzzles that are both fun and easy to accomplish. Soon, you'll become a part of the interesting history of jigsaw puzzles.

Appendix:
Patterns

This section contains dozens of patterns to augment your
puzzle making—including practice puzzles to help you get
the hang of cutting pieces, and also fancy figure templates
for you to use.

I've included three practice puzzle patterns to help
you start from the very beginning, if you wish. To use,
photocopy a pattern and affix it to a piece of puzzle wood
with adhesive spray. Cut on the lines to get an idea of what
scrolling puzzle pieces should feel like. Start with the large
puzzle, then progress to the medium, and finally to the
small. When you can cut the small puzzle with confidence,
you're ready to move on to the patternless practice puzzles
on page 32.

I've also created a library of fancy figures for you to
place on your own special-occasion puzzles. Symbols from
holidays, pets, nature, and more are included to make your
puzzles extra special. Refer to pages 64–65 or 75–76 for
instructions on how to incorporate a fancy figure into your
puzzle design.

These patterns are also available on the following website:
www.scrollsawer.com/jigsaw.

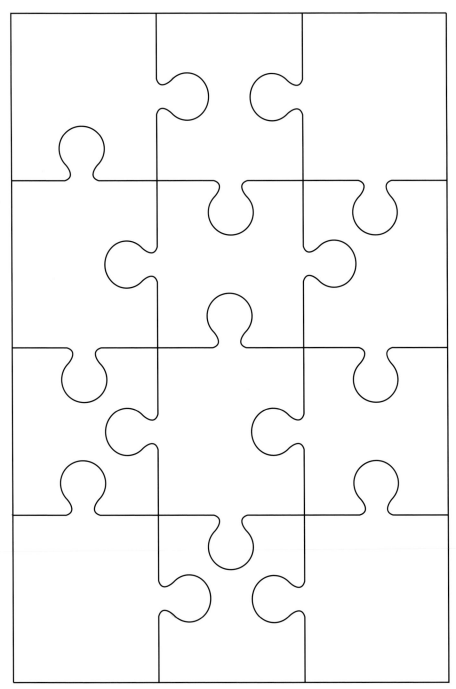

Large practice puzzle.
Photocopy at 100%.

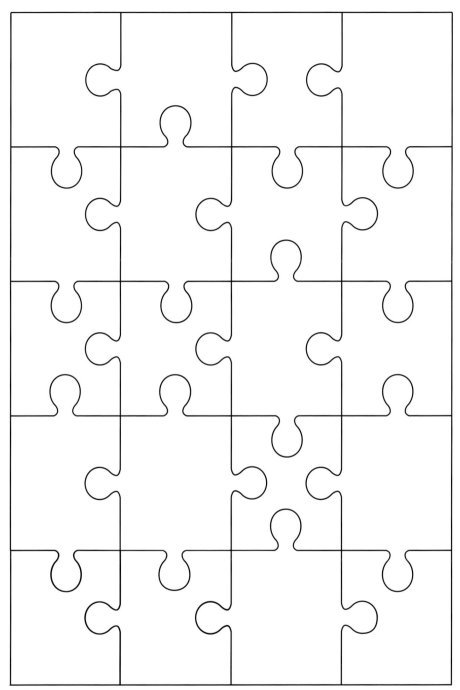

Medium practice puzzle.
Photocopy at 100%.

Small practice puzzle.
Photocopy at 100%.

Alphabet

Alphabet and Numbers (continued)

Numbers

Animals

Cat

Dog

Dolphin

Rabbit

Duck

Nature

Apple

Butterfly

Palm tree

Maple leaf

Tulip

Pear

Snowflake

Special Occasions

Baby bottle

Baby rattle

Graduation cap

Teddy bear

Christmas tree

Menorah

Gift

Special Occasions *(continued)*

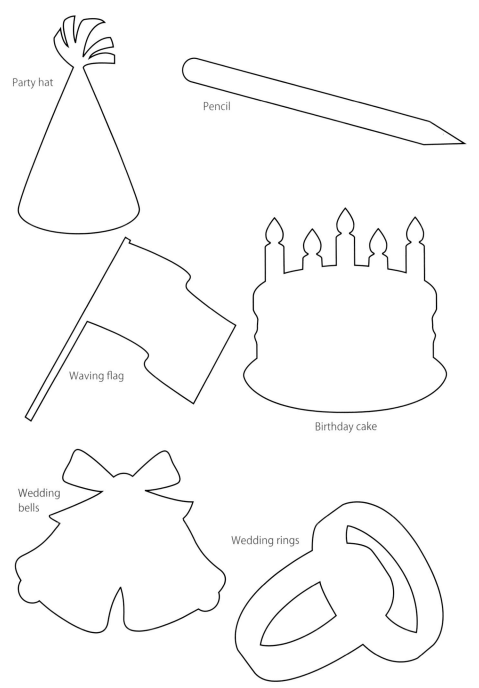

Party hat

Pencil

Waving flag

Birthday cake

Wedding
bells

Wedding rings

Shapes

Heart

Star

Transportation

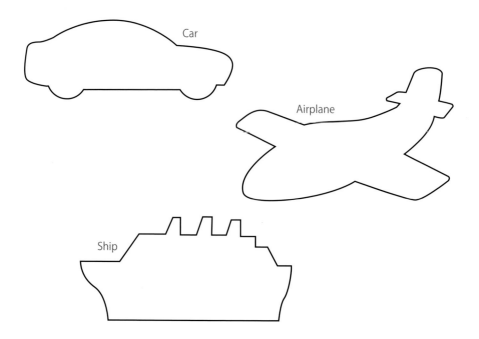

Car

Airplane

Ship

Appendix:
Index

adhesives, 24–25
backing materials, 23
blades, 12–15, 34–35, 63
blanks
  backing materials, 23
  choosing, 35
  cutting step-by-step. *See* step-by-step project
  preparing, step-by-step, 27
  sectioning, practice puzzle, 47–50
  sizing, 26
book overview, 6–7
books, for images, 22
bowl to catch pieces, 17
boxing puzzle, 82–86
breaks, taking, 34, 44, 58, 77
bristle brush, 39
cleaning pieces, 17, 81
copyright considerations, 20
cutting pieces, 34–38. *See also* pieces; practice puzzles; step-by-step project
  about: blades and, 12–15, 34–35; changing blades and, 63, 72; fatigue, breaks and, 34, 44, 58, 77
  adding interlocking tabs, 28
  along color lines, 30
  choosing blanks, 35
  drop outs, 30
  fancy figures, 29, 38, 71, 75–76, 79–80. *See also* patterns
  faux edge pieces, 31, 76, 78
  hiding corners, 28–29, 81
  interlocks and knobs, 28, 36–38, 59
  irregular puzzle shapes and, 30
  losing rows and, 65
  obscuring edge pieces, 28
  ocean wave cut, 73, 77–78
  problems and solutions, 39
  to resemble each other, 31
  smaller, 31
  spacing interlocks, 48
  unique interlocks, 30
  visualizing before, 35–36
design philosophy, 28–31. *See also* cutting pieces
drop outs, 30
dust removal, 17, 81
equipment, 12–17
  bowl to catch pieces, 17
  bristle brush, 39
  dust-removal sieve, 17
  lighting and eye protection, 15–16
  magnifier, 39
  nail clippers, 39
  scroll saws and blades, 12–15
  seating, 16–17

eye protection, 16
fancy figures, 29, 38, 71, 75–76, 79–80. *See also* patterns
fatigue, breaks and, 34, 44, 58, 77
faux edge pieces, 31, 76, 78
freehand style
  large, practice puzzle, 61–67
  small, practice puzzle, 55–60
fret saw, 89
glue and toothpick, 39
glues, 24–25
history of jigsaw puzzles, 88–92
images
  choosing, 18
  copyright considerations, 20
  heirloom puzzle ideas, 20
  paper stock for, 19, 21
  printing, 20–21
  sources of, 19–22
interlocks and knobs, 28, 36–38, 59
irregular puzzle shapes, 30
knobs. *See* interlocks and knobs
labeling puzzle, 85
lighting, 15–16
lithographs, as images, 21
losing rows, 65
magazine or catalog covers, as images, 21
magnifier, 39
maps, as images, 21–22
materials, 23–25
nail clippers, 39
ocean wave cut, 73, 77–78
paper stock, 19, 21
patterns, 93–102
  about: overview of, 93
  alphabet, 97
  animals, 98
  large, medium, small practice puzzles, 94–96
  nature, 99
  numbers, 98
  shapes, 102
  special occasions, 100–101
  transportation, 102
philosophy, of designing puzzles, 28–31. *See also* cutting pieces
photos, as images, 20–21
picture of completed puzzle, 85–86
pieces. *See also* cutting pieces
  cleaning dust from, 17, 81
  interlocks and knobs, illustrated, 28
  problems and solutions, 39
plywood, for backing, 23
practice puzzles, 40–67
  about: materials and preparation, 40; overview of, 40
  large freehand style, 61–67
  sectioning puzzle blanks, 47–50
  small freehand style, 55–60

stair-step cutting, 51–54
strip cutting method, 42–46
printing images, 20–21
scroll saws
  blades for, 12–15, 34–35, 63
  changing blades, 63, 72
  features and using, 12
seating, 16–17
sieve, for dust removal, 17
stair-step cutting, 51–54, 74, 77, 80
step-by-step project, 68–81
  about: changing blade and, 72; number of pieces, 68; overview of, 68; taking breaks, 77
  assembling equipment, 70
  assembling puzzle, 81
  boxing/labeling puzzle, 82–86
  choosing blank, 68, 70
  cleaning pieces, 81
  cutting blank in half, 71
  cutting halves in half, 71
  cutting pieces, 72–81
  fancy figures, 71, 75–76, 79–80. *See also* patterns
  faux edge pieces, 76, 78
  final thoughts, 86–87
  hiding corners, 81
  including picture or not, 85–86
  ocean wave cut, 73, 77–78
  planning puzzle, 70, 72
  stair-step cuts, 74, 77, 80
strip cutting method, 42–46
techniques and exercises. *See also* cutting pieces; practice puzzles; step-by-step project
  overview of, 32
  problems and solutions, 39

ACQUISITION EDITOR
Peg Couch

BOOK EDITOR
Kerri Landis

COPYEDITOR
Paul Hambke

COVER PHOTOGRAPHER
Scott Kriner

DESIGNERS
Chanyn Wise
Cheryl Lockley
Lindsay Hess

EDITORIAL ASSISTANT
Heather Stauffer

INDEXER
Jay Kreider

PROOFREADER
Lynda Jo Runkle

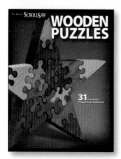
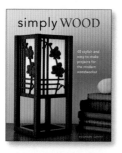
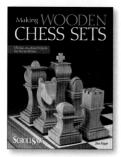